ISLAM
&
MODERNITY

Publications of the Center for Middle Eastern Studies, Number 15
Richard L. Chambers, General Editor

*1. Beginnings of Modernization in the Middle East: The Nineteenth Century
Edited by William R. Polk and Richard L. Chambers
2. The Mosque in Early Ottoman Architecture
By Aptullah Kuran
*3. Economic Development and Regional Cooperation: Kuwait
By Ragaei El Mallakh
*4. Studies in the Social History of Modern Egypt
By Gabriel Baer
5. Conflicts and Tensions in Islamic Jurisprudence
By Noel J. Coulson
6. The Modern Arabic Literary Language
By Jaroslav Stetkevych
*7. Iran: Economic Development under Dualistic Conditions
By Jahangir Amuzegar and M. Ali Fekrat
8. The Economic History of Iran, 1800–1914
By Charles Issawi
9. The Sense of Unity: The Sufi Tradition in Persian Architecture
By Nader Ardalan and Laleh Bakhtiar
10. The Forgotten Frontier: A History of Sixteenth-Century Ibero-American Frontier
By Andrew C. Hess
11. Muslim National Communism in the Soviet Union: A Revolutionary Strategy for the Colonial World
By Alexandre A. Bennigsen and S. Enders Wimbush
12. Karim Khan Zand: A History of Iran, 1747–1779
By John R. Perry
13. The Economic History of Turkey, 1800–1914
By Charles Issawi
14. Tribe and State in Bahrain
By Fuad I. Khuri
15. Islam and Modernity: Transformation of an Intellectual Tradition
By Fazlur Rahman

ISLAM & MODERNITY

Transformation of an Intellectual Tradition

Fazlur Rahman

The University of Chicago Press
Chicago & London

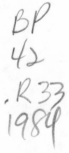

The University of Chicago Press, Chicago 60637
The University of Chicago Press, Ltd., London

 Published 1982
Paperback edition 1984
Printed in the United States of America
90 89 88 87 86 5 4 3

Library of Congress Cataloging in Publication Data

Rahman, Fazlur, 1919–
Islam & modernity.

(Publications of the Center for Middle Eastern Studies; no. 15)
Includes bibliographical references and index.
1. Islam—Education. 2. Koran—Hermeneutics. 3. Islam—History. I. Title. II. Title: Islam and modernity. III. Series.
BP42.R33 297′.122601 82-2720
ISBN 0-226-70283-9 (cloth) AACR2
ISBN 0-226-70284-7 (paper)

For
Bilqis,
my model of womanhood,
and
our children,
who are the joy of our life

Contents

Prefatory Note
ix

Introduction
1

1
The Heritage
13

2
Classical Islamic Modernism and Education
43

3
Contemporary Modernism
84

4
Prospects and Some Suggestions
130

Index
163

Prefatory Note

I began writing this book in 1977 and completed it in 1978, although I have noted certain subsequent developments at the revision stage. Here I want to record that two Pakistani intellectuals, Abū'l-Aʿlā Mawdūdī and Ishtiāq Ḥusain Qureshī, passed away in September 1979 and in January 1981. Their departure is a loss to Islam, despite my severe, and I believe perfectly justified, criticism of them.

Introduction

The following pages are the result of a research project undertaken at the University of Chicago and funded by the Ford Foundation in Islamic Education. This project, which was originally conceived as part of a much larger project entitled "Islam and Social Change," directly involved a dozen young scholars besides its co-directors, myself and Professor Leonard Binder. While the younger scholars have undertaken to write monographs on the various Muslim countries they have studied in this project, I have decided to write a general work on the medieval Islamic educational system, with its major features and deficiencies, and on the modernization efforts undertaken during the past century or so. In the last chapter I have tried to delineate certain general lines along which I believe these efforts should proceed in order to be really fruitful.

As the reader will see, by "Islamic education" I do not mean physical or quasi-physical paraphernalia and instruments of instruction such as the books taught or the external educational structure, but what I call "Islamic intellectualism"; for to me this is the essence of higher Islamic education. It is the growth of a genuine, original, and adequate Islamic thought that must provide the real criterion for judging the success or failure of an Islamic educational system. The reader will also be struck by my preoccupation with the correct method of interpreting the Qur'ān and may well wonder, at first sight, why this question should stand at the center of Islamic intellectualism. The answer is that the Qur'ān, for Muslims, is the divine word literally revealed to the Prophet Muḥammad (between 710 and 732 C.E.) in a sense in which probably no other religious document is held to be so. Further, the Qur'ān declares itself to be the most comprehensive guidance for man, both assuming and subsuming earlier revelations (12:111, 10:37, 6:114). Furthermore, the Qur'ānic revelation and the prophetic career of Muḥammad lasted for just over twenty-two years, during which period all kinds of decisions on policy in peace and in war, on legal and moral issues in private and public life were made in the face of actual situations; thus the Qur'ān had from the time of its revelation a practical and political application; it was not a *mere* devotional or personal pietistic text; Muḥammad's prophetic career was likewise geared toward the moral improvement of man in a concrete and communal sense, rather than toward the private and metaphysical. This naturally encouraged the Muslim jurists and intellectuals to look upon the Qur'ān (and the model of the Prophet) as a unique repository of answers to all sorts of questions. That this approach succeeded in practice further strengthened the original belief of the Muslims in the efficacy of the revelation in providing true answers to virtually all situations.

But the basic questions of method and hermeneutics were not squarely addressed by Muslims. The medieval systems of Islamic law worked fairly successfully partly because of the realism shown by the very early generations, who took the raw materials for this law from the customs and institutions of the conquered lands, modified them, where necessary, in the light of the Qur'ānic teaching, and integrated them with that teaching. Where interpreters attempted to deduce law from the Qur'ān in abstracto—for example, in the area of the penal law called *ḥudūd*—results were not very satisfactory. This is because the instrument for deriving law and other social institutions, called *qiyās,* or analogical reasoning, was not perfected to the requisite degree. The imperfection and imprecision of these tools was due in turn to the lack of an adequate method for understanding the Qur'ān itself, as I shall detail below. There was a general failure to understand the underlying unity of the Qur'ān, coupled with a practical insistence upon fixing on the words of various verses in isolation. The result of this "atomistic" approach was that laws were often derived from verses that were not at all legal in intent.

For the failure to understand the Qur'ān as a deeper unity yielding a definite weltanschauung, the greatest penalty was paid in the realm of theological thought. Whereas in the field of law, in the relative absence of such an internally discovered unity, the incorporation of foreign materials introduced a sufficient degree of practicality, the same process of adopting foreign ideas in the field of theology—again, in the absence of such a unitary vision of the Qur'ānic weltanschauung—proved disastrous, at least in the case of Ashʿarism, the dominant Sunni theology throughout medieval Islam. When this Sunni theological system collided in the twelfth century C.E. with the out-and-out rational-philosophical metaphysics of the Muslim philosophers (who had erected their thought system on the basis of Greek philosophy but had nevertheless made serious efforts to accommodate Islamic orthodoxy), the former well-nigh crushed the latter by its sheer weight. Subsequently philosophy took refuge and developed in a Shīʿī intellectual-spiritual milieu or was transformed into intellectual Sufism.

The philosophers, and often the Sufis, did understand the Qur'ān as a unity, but this unity was imposed upon the Qur'ān (and Islam in general) from without rather than derived from a study of the Qur'ān itself. Certain thought systems and thought orientations were adopted from outside sources (not necessarily wholly antagonistic to the Qur'ān but certainly alien to and not infrequently incompatible with it), adapted somewhat to the Islamic mental milieu, and expressed mostly in Islamic terminology, but this thin veneer could not hide the fact that their basic structure of ideas was not drawn from within the Qur'ān itself.

It is this more or less artificial Islamic character of these intellectual constructs—be it Ibn Sīnā's philosophy or Ibn ʿArabī's mysticism—that invited the severe attack by the representatives of Islamic orthodoxy. Despite the inner weakness and inadequacy of the orthodox system itself—particularly of the Ashʿarite theology, which, in its cardinal tenets of the inefficacy of the human will and purposelessness of the divine law, was in conflict with the Qur'ān—it was nevertheless not difficult for an al-Ghazālī or an Ibn Taymiya (and several others) to locate the basic discrepancy between Ibn Sīnā's metaphysics or Ibn ʿArabī's theosophy and the Islamic teaching. The upshot of this is that Islamic intellectualism has remained truncated.

This piecemeal, ad hoc, and often quite extrinsic treatment of the Qur'ān has not ceased in modern times; indeed, in some respects it has worsened. The pressures exerted by modern ideas and forces of social change, together with the colonial interregnum in Muslim lands, has brought about a situation in which the adoption of certain key modern Western ideas and institutions is resolutely defended by some Muslims and often justified through the Qur'ān, the wholesale rejection of modernity is vehemently advocated by others, and the production of "apologetic" literature that substitutes self-glorification for reform is virtually endless. Against this background the evolving of some adequate hermeneutical method seems imperative. Such a method, in my view, involves certain factors and excludes certain others: it is exclusively concerned with the cognitive aspect of the revelation and not with its aesthetic-appreciative or power-appreciative aspects. All revelation is a work of art and inspires a sense of the beautiful and a sense of awesome majesty (in Sufi terminology *jamāl* and *jalāl*). But above all it inspires that irreducible attitude of the mind called faith, which is both captivating and demanding. The Qur'ān is preeminently so. But the method of Qur'ānic hermeneutics I am talking about is concerned with an understanding of its message that will enable those who have faith in it and want to live by its guidance—in both their individual and collective lives—to do so coherently and meaningfully. In this purely cognitive effort both Muslims and, in certain areas, non-Muslims can share, provided the latter have the necessary sympathy and sincerity; but faith, which provides the motivation necessary to live by it, is of course characteristic only of those who are genuine Muslims. I do not deny that faith may be born out of this cognitive effort itself or that, more patently, faith may and ought to lead to such a cognitive effort, but the point is that pure cognition and emotive faith can be practically separated.

When I talk about "pure cognition" this does not mean cognition of historical facts to the exclusion of values; on the contrary, my central preoccupation is precisely with values—their meaning and their interpretation. But a cognition of *historical* values is also possible, with an adequate understanding, but without necessarily involving faith (although, of course, faith may be generated through an understanding of values, if that faith is not simply dogmatic). However my use of the term "historical values" must also be made clear. All values that are properly moral—and it is these with which we shall be concerned—have also an extrahistorical, "transcendental" being, and their location at a point in history does not exhaust their practical impact or, one might even say, their meaning. This category of values is different from certain other categories—for example, purely economic values. A certain economic value, represented by a certain society at a certain past time, exhausts its life within that socioeconomic context, and its meaning does not overflow that context; but not so with a moral value.

The process of interpretation proposed here consists of a double movement, from the present situation to Qur'ānic times, then back to the present. The Qur'ān is the divine response, through the Prophet's mind, to the moral-social situation of the Prophet's Arabia, particularly to the problems of the commercial Meccan society of his day. The Qur'ān, quite early, speaks of a "burden that was breaking your back," which was relieved by the revelation (94:1–3). The revelation, of course entailed a further "burdensome call" (73:5). The early suras of the Qur'ān make it abundantly clear that the acute problems in that society were polytheism (idol worship), exploitation of the poor, malpractices in trade, and general irresponsibility toward society (which there is good reason to believe the Qur'ān perceived as interconnected). The Qur'ān put forward the idea of a unique God to whom all humans are responsible and the goal of eradication of gross socioeconomic inequity. Qur'ānic theology and moral and legal teachings then gradually unfolded themselves in the political arena: the Meccans' rejection of Muḥammad's message, the protracted debates that followed, and later, in the Medinan phase of his life, the controversy waged against Jews and to some extent against Christians formed the backdrop against which the Qur'ān was revealed.

We see, then, that the Qur'ān and the genesis of the Islamic community occurred in the light of history and against a social-historical background. The Qur'ān is a response to that situation, and for the most part it consists of moral, religious, and social pronouncements that respond to specific problems confronted in concrete historical situations. Sometimes the Qur'ān simply gives an answer to a question or a problem, but usually these answers are stated in terms of an explicit or semiexplicit *ratio legis*, while there are also certain general laws enunciated from time to time. But, even where simple answers are given, it is possible to understand their reasons and hence deduce general laws by studying the background materials, which for the most part have been fairly intelligibly presented by the commentators.

The first of the two movements mentioned above, then, consists of two steps. First, one must understand the import or meaning of a given statement by studying the historical situation or problem to which it was the answer. Of course, before coming to the study of specific texts in the light of specific situations, a general study of the macrosituation in terms of society, religion, customs, and institutions, indeed, of life as a whole in Arabia on the eve of Islam and particularly in and around Mecca—not excluding the Perso-Byzantine Wars—will have to be made. The first step of the first movement, then, consists of understanding the meaning of the Qurʾān as a whole as well as in terms of the specific tenets that constitute responses to specific situations. The second step is to generalize those specific answers and enunciate them as statements of general moral-social objectives that can be "distilled" from specific texts in light of the sociohistorical background and the often-stated *rationes legis*. Indeed, the first step—the understanding of the meaning of the specific text—itself implies the second step and will lead to it. Throughout this process due regard must be paid to the tenor of the teaching of the Qurʾān as a whole so that each given meaning understood, each law enunciated, and each objective formulated will cohere with the rest. The Qurʾān as a whole does inculcate a definite attitude toward life and does have a concrete weltanschauung; it also claims that its teaching has "no inner contradiction" but coheres as a whole.

I shall presently remark upon the nature and the feasibility of this task of understanding. I should note here, however, that (besides language, grammar, style, etc.) a study of the views of Muslims—most particularly those of the earliest generations—will be helpful. But these views must occupy a secondary place to the objective materials outlined above, since historical interpretations of the Qurʾān, although they will be of help, are also to be judged by the understanding gained from the Qurʾān itself. There are several reasons for this: first, little attempt has ever been made to understand the Qurʾān as a unity; further, with the passage of time and the rise, growth, and hardening of different points of view and preconceived notions, subjective interpretations have multiplied. The historical tradition will therefore be more an object of judgment for the new understanding than an aid to it, although this historical traditional product can undoubtedly yield insights.

Whereas the first movement has been from the specifics of the Qur'ān to the eliciting and systematizing of its general principles, values, and long-range objectives, the second is to be from this general view to the specific view that is to be formulated and realized *now.* That is, the general has to be embodied in the present concrete sociohistorical context. This once again requires the careful study of the present situation and the analysis of its various component elements so we can assess the current situation and change the present to whatever extent necessary, and so we can determine priorities afresh in order to implement the Qur'ānic values afresh. To the extent that we achieve both moments of this double movement successfully, the Qur'ān's imperatives will become alive and effective once again. While the first task is primarily the work of the historian, in the performance of the second the instrumentality of the social scientist is obviously indispensable, but the actual "effective orientation" and "ethical engineering" are the work of the ethicist.

This second moment will also act as a corrective of the results of the first, that is, of understanding and interpretation. For if the results of understanding fail in application now, then either there has been a failure to assess the present situation correctly or a failure in understanding the Qur'ān. For it is not possible that something that could be and actually was realized in the specific texture of the past, cannot, allowing for the difference in the specifics of the present situation, be realized in the present context—where "allowing for the difference in the specifics of the present situation" includes both changing the rules of the past in conformity with the altered situation of the present (provided this changing does not violate the general principles and values derived from the past) and changing the present situation, where necessary, so it is brought into conformity with these general principles and values. Both tasks imply intellectual *jihād,* the second implying also a moral jihād or endeavor in addition to the intellectual.

The intellectual endeavor or jihād, including the intellectual elements of both the moments—past and present—is technically called *ijtihād,* which means "the effort to understand the meaning of a relevant text or precedent in the past, containing a rule, and to alter that rule by extending or restricting or otherwise modifying it in such a manner that a new situation can be subsumed under it by a new solution." This definition itself implies that a text or precedent can be generalized as a principle and that the principle can then be formulated as a new rule. This implies that the meaning of a past text or precedent, the present situation, and the intervening tradition can be sufficiently objectively known and that the tradition can be fairly objectively brought under the judgment of the (normative) meaning of the past under whose impact the tradition arose. It follows from this that tradition can be studied with adequate historical objectivity and separated not only from the present but also from the normative factors that are supposed to have generated it.

In modern hermeneutical theory, the "objectivity school" has insisted that one must first of all ascertain the meaning intended by the mind that authored the object of study. According to E. Betti, a contemporary representative of this school, the process of understanding is a "reversal" of the original creative process: the forms that we try to understand and interpret now are to be led back to the creative mind whose original contents they were, not as isolated items but as a coherent whole, and made to live again in the mind of the understanding subject.[1] It should be pointed out, however, that this unity of forms cannot be attributed simply to the mind; one must also consider the situation to which it is a response. This, of course, admits of varying degrees, but certainly, in the case of the Qur'ān, the objective situation is a sine qua non for understanding, particularly since, in view of its absolute normativity for Muslims, it is literally God's response through Muḥammad's mind (this latter factor has been radically underplayed by the Islamic orthodoxy) to a historic situation (a factor likewise drastically restricted by the Islamic orthodoxy in a real understanding of the Qur'ān).

The view of the "objectivity" school has been criticized by Hans Georg Gadamer in the work cited above as "psychologism" and as subjective. While it is true that representatives of this school often speak as though the being of ideas in the author's mind is crucial to understanding them (cf. Betti's view described above,

1. Cited in Hans Georg Gadamer, *Truth and Method* (New York: Seabury Press, 1975), p. 465.

where he seeks to trace back ideas to the original mind in order to understand them as a true unity, whereas I have contended that the invisible context of ideas is not just mental but environmental as well), they surely do not conceive of ideas only as mental events; for while their occurrence is in a mind, their *intentio* or meaning is "referred" outside the mind. Against this view, Gadamer maintains his phenomenological doctrine according to which all experience of understanding presupposes a preconditioning of the experiencing subject and therefore, without due acknowledgment of this fact of being predetermined (which is the essence of Gadamer's entire hermeneutical theory), any attempt to understand anything is doomed to unscientific vitiation. What so predetermines me as an understanding subject is what Gadamer calls "the effective history," that is, not only the historical influence of the object of investigation, but the totality of other influences that make up the very texture of my being. Thus there is no question of any "objective" understanding of anything at all. Even when we become aware of this predetermination—that is, develop an "effective-historical consciousness" as distinguished from ordinary "historical consciousness"—the former is so limited that it cannot overcome this preconditioning. It is, of course, clear that this doctrine is radically opposed to what I have contended above by way of the hermeneutics of the Qur'ān. If Gadamer's thesis is correct, then the double-movement theory I have put forward has no meaning at all. No wonder a thinker like Betti rejects Gadamer's view as hopelessly subjective.

"Obviously the burden of my argument," writes Gadamer, "is that this quality of being determined by effective-history still dominates the modern historical and scientific consciousness and that beyond any possible knowledge of this domination. The effective-historical consciousness is so radically finite that our whole being, achieved in the totality of our destiny, inevitably transcends its knowledge of itself."[2] Again, "In fact history does not belong to us, but we belong to it. Long before we understand ourselves through the process of self-examination, we understand ourselves in a self-evident way in the family, society and state in which we live. . . . The self-awareness of the individual is only a flickering in the closed circuits of historical life."[3] The

2. Ibid., p. xxii.
3. Ibid., p. 245.

task of philosophical hermeneutics is to clarify precisely this predetermination; hence, "from the viewpoint of philosophical hermeneutics, the contrast between historical and dogmatic method has no absolute validity."[4]

The principle of effective history stated blandly, of course, will not work. It is obvious that there have been changes in human traditions, sometimes radical. In Christianity, the effective history of a fifth-century Augustine, a thirteenth-century Aquinas, and a sixteenth-century Luther could not have been quite the same; but what is even more important than that is that the conscious thought product of those men brought vast and vital changes into the subsequent effective history. So is the case with a tenth-century al-Ashʿarī, an eleventh-century al-Ghazālī, and a fourteenth-century Ibn Taymiya: Islamic tradition was never the same again after the conscious activity of each and all of them. Every critique or modification of a tradition involves a consciousness of what is being criticized or rejected and hence, to that extent, self-awareness. In view of the revolutionary changes wrought by some men in their traditions, it is therefore not proper to say that "the self-awareness of the individual is only a flickering in the closed circuits of historical life." It is also untenable to say that their responses were predetermined, and primarily by their effective histories. What seems reasonable to hold is that all conscious responses to the past involve two moments that must be distinguished. One is the objective ascertaining of the past (—which Gadamer does not allow), which is possible in principle provided requisite evidence is available; the other is the response itself, which necessarily involves values and which is determined (not predetermined) by my present situation, of which effective history is a part but of which my conscious effort and self-aware activity also constitute an important part. For Gadamer these two moments are utterly inseparable and indistinguishable.

By his statement that there is no absolute contrast between the historical and the dogmatic methods, Professor Gadamer wants to say that both are limited by the effective-historical element but that both are able to question tradition, there being only a difference of degree between the two. One might point out that questioning in the historical method is the questioning of *histor-*

4. Ibid., p. xxi.

ical facts, since by definition and as an ideal it does not concern itself with values, whereas questioning in the dogmatic method is primarily the questioning of traditional values. First of all, it is highly doubtful if even in the "dogmatic" questioning process some "historical" consciousness in not involved, since the fact that the tradition is the tradition *of the past* presupposes some "historical" distance. But, more important, one wonders if the term "dogmatic" is proper in this context, since what Gadamer has characterized as the "dogmatic" (i.e., nonhistorical or prehistorical) method of questioning tradition emerges on closer examination as a "rational" method of questioning. When Augustine or Luther questioned their traditions, their questioning was within the dogmatic field, but surely their method of questioning was rational—that is, they believed that certain parts of their tradition were incompatible with and contradictory to other more basic parts of that tradition. Here, then, in place of the "historical" distance or space, a rational space mediates between the past and the present, although, as I have said, a historical consciousness is not lacking completely but perhaps is present as a secondary phenomenon.

Thus if one asks, "What is the predetermining effective history of a certain tradition?" there is no straightforward answer, since it depends on an answer to the further question, "For whom?" In the case of a consciousness that has been able to work deliberate change in that tradition, the answer would be, "the tradition minus the change that that particular consciousness has wrought." This means that the process of questioning and changing a tradition—in the interests of preserving or restoring its normative quality in the case of its normative elements—can continue indefinitely and that there is no fixed or privileged point at which the predetermining effective history is immune from such questioning and then being consciously confirmed or consciously changed. This is what is required for an adequate hermeneutical method of the Qurʾān, as I have outlined it herein.

1

The Heritage

The Qur᾽ān and the Prophet

When one reviews the performance of Muḥammad as a religious leader and studies the Qur᾽ān closely as the document of his revelatory experiences, one cannot fail to perceive that an inner unity and an unmistakable sense of direction—despite the multitude of different historical situations faced and exigencies met—are displayed in the Prophet's activity and the Qur᾽ānic guidance. I am, of course, talking not of the actual effect this teaching had upon Muḥammad's early or late followers, the treatment of which will follow this section, but of the nature and the quality of this teaching, viewed in its setting, with reference to its historical context on the one hand and the personality of the Prophet on the other. In this section I will be concerned with this teaching in its major features and this performance in its bold outlines, rather than with the minutiae of details, in order to bring out their originality and their potentialities.[1]

It seems certain that, because of their mutual involvement and interdependence, the doctrines of the One Creator-Sustainer God, of the necessity of socioeconomic justice, and of the Last Judgment were elements of the original religious experience of Muḥammad. As this experience unfolds under the general refusal of the Meccans to accept his teaching the idea of a judgment

1. See my book *Major Themes of the Qur᾽ān* (Chicago and Minneapolis: Bibliotheca Islamica, 1980).

in history upon nations in accordance with the quality of their collective behavior originates and gains steady strength in the middle and some years of the last Meccan periods. In fact, it almost overshadows that of the Last Judgment until Medina, where, owing to the new opportunities of the task of constructing an ethically based sociopolitical order, accounts of divine judgment upon earlier nations and their fates are no longer called for. Yet the idea of a universal judgment continues. Although both God consciousness and the conviction of the Last Day are powerful and persistent themes in the Qurʾān, there is no doubt that belief in God and human accountability play a strictly functional role there. The central concern of the Qurʾān is the conduct of man. Just as in Kantian terms no ideal knowledge is possible without the regulative ideas of reason (like first cause), so in Qurʾānic terms no real morality is possible without the regulative ideas of God and the Last Judgment. Further, their very moral function requires that they exist for religiomoral experience and cannot be mere intellectual postulates to be "believed in." God is the transcendent anchoring point of attributes such as life, creativity, power, mercy, and justice (including retribution) and of moral values to which a human society must be subject if it is to survive and prosper—a ceaseless struggle for the cause of the good. This constant struggle is the keynote of man's normative existence and constitutes the service (*ʿibāda*) to God with which the Qurʾān squarely and inexorably charges him.

But the substantive or "constitutive"—as Kantian phraseology would have it—teaching of the Prophet and the Qurʾān is undoubtedly *for action in this world,* since it provides guidance for man concerning his behavior on earth in relation to other men. God exists in the mind of the believer to regulate his behavior if he is religiomorally experienced, but that which is to be regulated is the essence of the matter. The bane of later medieval Islam, as we shall presently see, was that what was regulative, namely, God, was made the exclusive object of experience and thus, instead of men's seeking values from this experience, the experience became the end in itself. Whether or not this experience had any other content—eminent Sufis themselves, like al-Ghazālī and al-Sirhindī, thought it had none, and this view seems to me both intelligible and correct—it was mostly either neutral to social morality or even negatively related to it. The intellectual efforts of Christian theologians to unravel the nature of God (as love) and the mysteries of the Trinity were empty formalism compared with the Sufi experience of God (for the latter at least had a positive and enriching influence on personaltiy building, though mostly individual and asocial). Nevertheless, the Christian theology had the beneficial effect of sharpening the mind, and therefore, when that mind later was applied to the natural world, it produced amazing results in the scientific field. But the bane of modernity, in the form of secularism, is far worse than that of either medieval Islamic Sufism or medieval Christian theology, since secularism destroys the sanctity and universality (transcendence) of all moral values—a phenomenon whose effects have just begun to make themselves felt, most palpably in Western societies. Secularism is necessarily atheistic. So far as the establishment of an ethically based social order is concerned—and this is the greatest desideratum of minkind today—the effects of medieval Islamic Sufism, of the Christian obsession with theology, or of modern secularism differ little.

How different and how morally invigorating are the concerns of the Qurʾān—for the Prophet, judging from both the Qurʾān and his Sunna (i.e., his exemplary conduct), was "God-intoxicated," and the Qurʾān itself certainly appears to be theocentric. But this deep God consciousness is creatively and organically related to the founding of an ethical sociopolitical order in the world, since, in the view of the Qurʾān, those who forget God eventually forget themselves (59:19), and their individual and corporate personalities disintegrate. It is this God consciousness that sent Muḥammad out of the Cave of Ḥirāʾ, where he was wont to contemplate, into the world, never to return to that cave—or the contemplative life—again. What issued from his experience in the cave was not merely the demolishing of a plurality of gods, but a sustained and determined effort to achieve socioeconomic justice. He aimed at constituting a community for goodness and justice in the world—what I have called an ethically based sociopolitical order "under God," that is, according to the principle that moral values cannot be made and unmade by man at his own whim or convenience and should not be misused or abused for the sake of expediency. Muḥammad tried to strengthen and enfranchise the weaker segments of society as well as to divest the privileged of their prerogatives in the religious field (the clergy), in the political field (autocratic or oligarchic rule), and in the socioeconomic field (undue economic or sex power). Mr. Maxime Rodinson has aptly characterized Muḥammad as a combination of Charlemagne, who spread Christianity among the Saxon tribes of Germans primarily so as to establish and consolidate an empire, and Jesus, whose kingdom "was not of this world."

When one studies the social aspect of Muḥammad's reform, two features appear striking. First, before introducing a major measure of social change, the ground was well prepared. Of course, in the sector of public legislation the Prophet did not have the power to act while he was in Mecca; it was only in Medina, where he had political and administrative authority, that he could legislate. Thus, although Qurʾānic warnings against usury were issued in Mecca, usury was not legally banned until the Prophet had been in Medina for some time. Similarly, emphatic statements concerning amelioration of the condition of the poor were made from the beginning of Islam (indeed, this coupled with the unity of God was the motive force for the genesis of the Islamic movement), but laws in this field, including the law of the *zakāt* tax, were not promulgated until well after the Prophet had settled in Medina, although the measure of "brotherhood" (*muwākhāt*) between the local population (*anṣār*) and the Meccan immigrants (*muhājirūn*) was taken soon after his arrival in Medina. Such instances militate against the liberal use of the "principle of graduation" in Qurʾānic legislation, so much exploited by later Muslim jurists and many present-day reformers. Nevertheless, it is beyond doubt that he made no precipitate decisions on important issues of public policy but awaited "the coming down of revelation." The Prophet was naturally a shy and reticent person and did not intrude into people's affairs so long as they ran smoothly—the portrayal of him by later juristic literature as ceaselessly coming forth with decision upon decision (more often than not contradictory!) on real or hypothetical questions is decidedly false. It goes without saying that he never gave decisions on purely hypothetical issues or on issues that were never brought to his notice. On the other hand, despite Muḥammad's reticence, an equally determined will unfailingly comes through, a will that spurns compromises on fundamental issues. One does not need to remind oneself that a man with this mixture of opposing mental traits and conscious of a "heavy mission," as the Qurʾān says, must be engaged in a constant inner dialectic—the ideal moral state for man to be in, according to the Qurʾān. The verses in sura 53, where the Prophet had reportedly made concessions to the goddesses of the Meccan pagans that were subsequently "abrogated," is, along with other Qurʾānic evidence, a direct proof of this phenomenon. The second side of the Prophet, his determination, finally won over his other side. If there were an artist in the world who could portray pure moral states, the Prophet's picture would emerge as most interesting, attractive, and significant.

The second all-important feature of the legislation of the Qurʾān is that it (like the decisions of the Prophet) always had a background or a historical context, which the Muslim commentators of the Qurʾān call "occasions of revelation." But the literature on the "occasions of revelation" is often highly contradictory and chaotic. The basic reason for this state of affairs seems to be that, although most Qurʾānic commentators were aware of the importance of these "situational contexts," either because of their historical significance or for their aid in understanding the point of certain injunctions, they never realized their full import, particularly from the second point of view. Instead, they enunciated the principle that "although an injunction might have been occasioned by a certain situation, it is nevertheless universal in its general application." This principle is sound enough provided it means by an "injunction" the value underlying that injunction and not merely its literal wording. But the value can be yielded only by understanding well not only the language, but above all the situational context of a given injunction. This, however, was generally not done, since, as I have just said, the real significance of the "occasions of revelation" was not realized. From the chaos reigning in the field (although there is some historical information on many important points as well) one can guess that, since these developments had occurred during their own lifetime, the Prophet's immediate followers—the Companions—did not care to record them or get them recorded, while later generations, although possessing a certain amount of reliable information, were left to guess at what these "occasions" might have been. Also, in their social and collective behavior Arabs, like all tribally organized societies, were highly custom-bound, and a set pattern of behavior (called Sunna) acquired sanctity for them—hence the intense and protracted opposition to Muḥammad, who broke this set pattern, often at its most sensitive points. Once an absolutely normative revealed document like the Qurʾān became established, however, given the habit of adherence to set patterns, the Arabs were naturally loath to deviate from its literal meaning. This largely explains the astounding degree of integrity of the Qurʾānic text over many centuries. There is no doubt that early scholars of Islam and leaders of the community exercised a good deal of freedom and ingenuity in interpreting the Qurʾān, including the principles of *ijtihād* (personal reasoning) and *qiyās* (analogical reasoning from a certain text of the Qurʾān and arguing on its basis to solve a new case or problem that has certain essential resemblances to the former). There was, however, no well-argued-out system of rules for these procedures, and early legal schools sometimes went too far in using this freedom. For this reason in the late eighth century C.E. al-Shāfiʿī successfully fought for the general acceptance of "traditions from the Prophet" as a basis for interpretation instead of ijtihād or qiyās. Yet the real solution lay only in understanding the Qurʾānic injunctions strictly in their context and background and trying to extrapolate the principles or values that lay behind the injunctions of the Qurʾān and the Prophetic Sunna. But this line was never developed systematically, at least by Muslim jurists.

In most cases, however, it is not difficult to see the real point of a verse or the basic import of a given injunction. The Qurʾān, for the most part, explicitly states why an order is being given or a statement or comment is being made, even though it rarely refers to a specific case by name. Thus in the case of *ribā* (usury), the actual case of those tribes who, burdened by incurable ribā debts, were threatening to cause trouble is not mentioned at all, yet the institution of ribā is denounced in the strongest possible terms as an abominable form of exploitation, and a threat of "war from God and His Messenger" is issued against those who do not desist from it. Even when the reason for a certain command is not explicitly stated, it is not difficult to guess it. If one peruses the inheritance verses, for example, it becomes clear that the Qurʾān is essentially extending the right of inheritance to women, who did not possess that right in pre-Islamic Arab law, and is therefore concerned with establishing those categories of relations who have a right to inheritance. But, second, it is also pointing out the usefulness of these potential inheritors to the propositus on the basis of kinship by saying, "You do not know whether your fathers are more beneficial to you or your sons" (4:11). Therefore, even though the Qur᾽ān seldom refers to actual events and situations and almost never mentions names, it would be inaccurate to characterize it as an esoteric document, for it is eminently possible to accurately determine the rationales behind its statements, comments, and injunctions.

The basic élan of the Qur᾽ān—the stress on socioeconomic justice and essential human egalitarianism—is quite clear from its very early passages. Now all that follows by way of Qur᾽ānic legislation in the field of private and public life, even the "five pillars" of Islam that are held to be religion par excellence, has social justice and the building of an egalitarian community as its end. To insist on a *literal* implementation of the rules of the Qur᾽ān, shutting one's eyes to the social change that has occurred and that is so palpably occurring before our eyes, is tantamount to deliberately defeating its moral-social purposes and objectives. It is just as though, in view of the Qur᾽ānic emphasis on freeing slaves, one were to insist on preserving the institution of slavery so that one could "earn merit in the sight of God" by freeing slaves. Surely the whole tenor of the teaching of the Qur᾽ān is that there should be no slavery at all. The sort of reasoning that would retain slavery is, of course, seldom employed by any intelligent and morally sensitive Muslim. But there is an argument used by the vast majority of Muslims, and indeed primarily by the majority of Muslim religious leaders, that is very similar in nature. It is that, since it is a "pillar" of Islam to pay zakāt levy, a tax the Qur᾽ān had imposed primarily (but by no means exclusively) on the rich for the welfare of the poor, *some people must remain poor in order for the rich to earn merit in the sight of God.* There is, of course, no society on earth in which there are no needy people, and in Islam the state, through its zakāt system, has to fulfill their needs; but an argument like this one seeks to give a decisive blow to the very orientation of the Qur᾽ān and provides the best kind of prop for the communist slogan that religion is the opiate of the masses. Or, again, to say that, no matter how much women may develop intellectually, their evidence must on principle carry less value than that of a man is an outrageous affront to the Qur᾽ān's purposes of social evolution—and so on.

Just as we can see the broad, humane principles of justice, mutual help, and mercy worked into the fabric of the Qur᾽ānic legislation, so, conversely, does the movement of the mind from the concrete legislation of the Qurʾān back to the general principles end up on the same broad principles that constituted its primary élan. Muslims, and particularly modernist Muslims, have often contended that the Qurʾān gives us "the principles" while the Sunna or our reasoning embodies these fundamentals in concrete solutions. This is considerably less than a half-truth and is dangerously misleading. If we look at the Qurʾān, it does not in fact give many general principles: for the most part it gives solutions to and rulings upon specific and concrete historical issues; but, as I have said, it provides, either explicitly or implicitly, the rationales behind these solutions and rulings, from which one *can deduce general principles.* In fact, this is the only sure way to obtain the real truth about the Qurʾānic teaching. One must generalize on the basis of Qurʾānic treatment of actual cases—taking into due consideration the sociohistorical situation then obtaining—since, although one can find some general statements or principles there, these for the most part are embedded in concrete treatments of actual issues, whence they must be disengaged. The net conclusion to be drawn from these considerations is the following. *In building any genuine and viable Islamic set of laws and institutions, there has to be a twofold movement: First one must move from the concrete case treatments of the Qurʾān—taking the necessary and relevant social conditions of that time into account—to the general principles upon which the entire teaching converges. Second, from this general level there must be a movement back to specific legislation, taking into account the necessary and relevant social conditions now obtaining.* The contention that certainty belongs not to the meanings of particular verses of the Qurʾān and their content (by "certainty" I mean not their revealed character, for undoubtedly the Qurʾān is revealed in its entirety, but the certainty of our understanding of their true meaning and import) but to the Qurʾān as a whole, that is, as a set of coherent principles or values where the total teaching will converge, might appear shocking to many Muslims who have been for centuries habituated to think of the laws of the Qurʾān in a discrete, atomistic, and totally unintegrated manner (even though the Qurʾān loudly proclaims that it is a highly integrated and cohesive body of teaching). The following statement of the famous Mālikī jurist al-Shāṭibī (d. 1388) should convince them not only of its reasonableness, but of its absolute necessity. After stating that eternal validity belongs only to the "general principles" (*uṣūl kulliya*) and not to the particulars of the Qur'ān, al-Shāṭibī goes on:

> This being so, i.e., that pure reason divorced from the Sharīʿa principles is unable to yield religiomoral values, reliance must be placed primarily on Sharīʿa proofs in deducing law. But according to their common use, these latter either have no certainty at all or very little—I mean when Sharīʿa proofs are taken one by one. This is because if these proofs are in the category of ḥadīths coming from single or isolated chains of transmission, it is obvious that they yield no certainty. But if these ḥadīths are traceable to an overwhelming number of chains of transmission [*mutawātir*], certainty with regard to them, i.e., their meaning, depends upon premises all or most of which are only conjectural. Now that which depends upon what is uncertain is inevitably itself uncertain as well. For a determination of their meaning depends upon the correct transmission of linguistic usage, grammatical opinions, etc.; thus taking all these factors into consideration the possibility of establishing with certainty the meaning of these ḥadīths is nil. Some jurists have taken refuge in the view that although these Sharīʿa proofs are in themselves uncertain, when they are supported by indirect evidence or concomitants [*qarā'in*] they can yield assurance. But this occurs rarely or not at all.
>
> The proofs considered reliable here are only those inducted from a number of conjectural proofs which *converge* upon an idea in such a manner that they can yield certainty, for a totality of proofs possesses a strength which separate and disparate proofs do not possess. This is the reason why an overwhelming tradition possesses certainty and this, i.e., the case under discussion here, is such a case. When through inducting from a whole range of conjectural proofs of a certain point a coherent totality emerges that can yield sure knowledge, that constitutes the desired proof. . . . It is in this way that the obligatoriness of the five principles—like prayer, Zakāt, etc.—has been absolutely established. Otherwise if someone were to argue for the obligatoriness of prayer basing himself only on God's repeated statements in the Qur'ān: 2:43, 83, 110; 4:77; 6:72 etc.; "And establish prayers," this kind of proof, taken by itself, would be open to several objections. But then this proof is supported all round by other indirect evidence and

well-ordered rules whereby the duty of prayer is rendered absolutely obligatory in religion, such that a person who doubts it is like one who doubts the very basis of religion. . . . When you consider why consensus is an irrefutable proof or a report from a single chain of transmission or reasoning by analogy *can become* an irrefutable proof, it is all reducible to this method. For in all these cases, i.e., a consensus, an isolated report or an analogy, proofs are adduced from places that are innumerable, and also they come from different kinds of sources which cannot be reduced to a single type. And yet they all converge upon one idea which is the object of all probative reasoning. Thus when various proofs concerning a certain matter abound and *are mutually corroborative,* through their total effect they produce certainty.

This is the case with sources of proofs used in this book—they are the sources whence principles are derived. But the earlier jurists often left this fact unmentioned and did not explicitly state it, so that some later jurists ignored it altogether. Consequently, arguing on the basis of individual verses of the Qur'ān and individual ḥadīths became difficult, since such a jurist did not argue on the basis of their *cumulative force.* Thus, the opponent was able to attack each individual textual proof separately and weakened its probative value in accordance with rules governing principles that are supposed to guide certainty. Yet, if these texts are taken in this way, i.e., in their totality and cumulative effect, there is no difficulty. But if the Sharīʿa proofs for general principles as well as particulars are taken as such an opponent takes them, we should be left without any certainty at all with regard to any Sharīʿa rule whatever—unless we bring in reason as a partner. Reason, however, can play its role only after the Sharīʿa bases are there. It is necessary, therefore, to follow this convergence principle in order to establish the fundamental proofs.[2]

Development of Islamic Disciplines

If I am correct in the criterion of true Islamicity I have laid down in the foregoing and have corroborated with a lengthy quotation from an eminent Muslim jurist, namely, that a doctrine

2. Al-Shāṭibī, *Kitāb al-Muwāfiqāt,* 4 vols. (Cairo: Muḥammad 'Alī Ṣabīḥ, 1969), 1:13–14.

or an institution is genuinely Islamic to the extent that it flows from the total teaching of the Qur'ān and the Sunna and hence successfully applies to an appropriate situation or satisfies a requirement, then it will not be Islamic to the extent that it does not flow from the teaching of the Qur'ān and the Sunna as a whole and hence will not solve a given problem or apply to a given situation Islamically. There are two ways such a body of teaching may be said to be applied as a whole to a given situation, be it social, political, or economic. First, someone may have lived through that teaching and thus have wholly internalized or ingested it so that, when a given situation presented itself, he judged the situation in the light of what he had ingested. The second method, intellectual in character in contradistinction to the first method, which may be called experiential, involves an analysis of that teaching in both historical and systematic terms; that is, it views the unfolding of the Qur'ān and the Sunna historically so as to understand their meaning and then systematically arranges values in order of priority and posteriority, subordinating the more particular to the more general and ultimate, and thus obtains an answer from this system for a given problem or a given situation.

After the death of the Prophet, and particularly when soon thereafter Muslims expanded outside the Arabian Peninsula and faced new administrative, juridical, and fiscal situations, their way of dealing with these situations was more like the first than the second method, although the second—the intellectually deliberative—was not totally lacking. This was only natural, for during the lifetime of the Prophet, although the more thinking minds among his Companions must have reflected on certain matters, he was there to give the necessary decisons. Hence at his death the Muslims inherited the Qur'ān and the prophet's example, but no detailed, intellectually worked-out system of thought. When new questions were referred to them, for example in Iraq or Egypt, they gave answers that, although taking into account local customs and practices, were based primarily upon the general teaching of the Qur'ān that they had actually lived through and by which their being had been permeated, rather than, in general, appealing to individual verses of the Qur'ān or texts of the Sunna, unless such verses had a clear-cut and direct bearing on the issue. Of course, even among the Companions of the Prophet, not everyone was of the same caliber or of the same depth of intimacy with the inner thinking of the Qurʾān and of the Prophet. The nucleus of the Prophet's followers consisted of relatively few poeple, and not every Companion was an ʿUmar or an ʿAlī or an Ibn Masʿūd.

It was for this reason then—because the men of the first generation of Islam gave judgments in the light of their experience of the Qurʾānic teaching as a whole—that they did not quote individual verses unless these had a direct bearing on the problem under question. It was, in fact, more to the point on their part to quote a concrete precedent from the Prophet's life, if one was available. Otherwise, they relied on the overall understanding of the purposes of the Qurʾān. A striking illustration is provided by ʿUmar's refusal after the conquest of Iraq to divide that land among the Muslim conquering soldiers as booty, in accordance with the Prophet's general practice within Arabia. ʿUmar's intuition was that the Prophet's practice concerning tribal territories was no longer practicable now that whole countries were being conquered. Under insistent pressure from the opposition, ʿUmar finally appealed to the Qurʾān 59:10 to buttress the stand he had taken without quoting any specific verse of the Qurʾān but in the interest of the general Qurʾānic demands for social justice and fair play. It was this kind of situation that led J. Schacht to make the astonishing statement in his *Origins of Muhammedan Jurisprudence* that in the early decision-making process in Islam, "the Qurʾān was invariably introduced at a secondary stage." If this statement means, as it apparently does, that Muslims *ignored* the Qurʾān in the first instance, it is unintelligible and absurd. But if it means that early Muslims acted first upon their experience of the totality of the Qurʾānic teaching and introduced the citation of particular verses only at a secondary stage, then this statement describes a phenomenon that is both natural and intelligible.

The most crucial stage in the development of the religious sciences is reached during the next two generations, the "Successors" and "Successors to the Successors." These two generations had not, of course, been witnesses to the unfolding of the Qurʾān and the Prophet's mission. Nevertheless there were among them those who excelled many of the Companions in intellectual acuteness; and, of course, they were extremely sincere men. It is during these early generations succeeding the Companions that the juristic genius of Muslims comes to fruition, and it seems certain that the oft-quoted alleged ḥadīth "May God make that person prosper who listens to what I say carefully and then transmits it faithfully to others, for many a transmitter is less good (or, no good) at understanding the meaning of my words compared with him to whom he might transmit it"[3] arose among certain circles of jurists of these generations. For it is quite obvious that this ḥadīth seeks to credit jurists with proper understanding as opposed to traditionists who merely transmit reports from the Prophet.

I have called this stage crucial because it was during this period that an appeal to individual verses of the Qur'ān and texts of Ḥadīth began to be made in order to resolve issues legally. If a sufficiently direct and obvious text was available, the matter was considered "settled" for good; if not, then a text had to be found that was close enough to the case under consideration so that the issue could be resolved on the basis of similarities, although allowing for differences. The first method was called *naṣṣ,* that is, decision on the basis of a "clear text," while the second, more complicated procedure was called *qiyās,* that is, analogical reasoning. The naṣṣ has traditionally been considered the surest ground for decisions and thought to be absolutely incontrovertible; yet the passage I quoted from al-Shāṭibī in the preceding section strongly contradicts this stand, for, according to al-Shāṭibī, no individual text by itself can have absolute probative force unless it is understood in the light of its historical background and the total relevant teaching of the Qur'ān and the Sunna. Indeed, al-Shaybānī, the second-century Ḥanafī jurist (d. 799) makes it plain that a certain text can become a naṣṣ, or textual proof, for more than one thing depending on how you understand the text, so that the potentially probative words become a "text depending upon what is understood from them."

As for qiyās, or analogical reasoning (the method most commonly employed by most Muslim jurists to derive law from the Qur'ān and the Sunna), its use in the first century and a half of Islam naturally led to chaotic results and a bewildering richness of legal opinions in Islam. If a "clear text" can yield more than one opinion, one can scarcely imagine how qiyās, which operates by analogy, could lead to any uniform legal results. If for one jurist a certain verse of the Qur'ān or a certain precedent

3. Fazlur Rahman, *Islamic Methodology in History* (Karachi: Islamic Research Institute, 1965), p. 45.

of the Prophet constituted the basis of analogical reasoning for a given case, for another jurist quite a different text or precedent offered a basis for analogical reasoning. If at this stage jurists had undertaken a systematic working out of the values and principles of the Qurʾān instead of working with such loose tools, the results might have been astonishingly different. Not that difference of opinion could have been eliminated—this is neither possible nor desirable—but at least differences would have been minimized, and, what is more, these differences would have occurred on more intelligible and justifiable grounds so that communication between different points of view would have become much easier. Instead, al-Shāfiʿī's (d. 819) contention that a ḥadīth, even though it be "isolated" and transmitted by only one transmissional chain, must be accepted as binding, and that in face of such a ḥadīth no reasoning can be allowed, had to be accepted because it provided an anchoring point in the midst of what seemed to be an interminable conflict of opinion. But even this proved inadequate, for already in al-Shāfiʿī's time and much more during the following century, a vast number of ḥadīths had become available reflecting and supporting the very differences of opinion to which al-Shāfiʿī's principle was supposed to put an end.

This proliferation of ḥadīths resulted in the cessation of an orderly growth in legal thought in particular and in religious thought in general. I say "orderly growth" because no functioning human society can be utterly static—some changes always continue to occur. But in the Muslim world these changes were neither controlled nor directed toward an end. Most modern Muslim thinkers have laid the blame for this relatively static state of affairs on the destruction of the caliphate in the mid-thirteenth century and the political disintegration of the Muslim world. But, as my preceding analysis has shown, the spirit of Islam had become essentially static long before that; indeed, this stagnation was inherent in the bases on which Islamic law was founded. The development of theology displays the same characteristics even more dramatically than does legal thought. This theology (*kalām*), which took shape during the tenth, eleventh, and twelfth centuries C.E., came to claim for itself the exalted function of being the "defender of the bases of Islamic law," in its most dominant and enduring form of Ashʿarism. As such it rejected causality and the efficacy of the human will in the interests of divine omnipotence (man was therefore only metaphorically an actor, the real actor being God alone), declared good and evil to be knowable only through the revelation (and not through natural reason), and denied that divine commandments in the Qurʾān had any purpose (they were rather to be obeyed solely because they were divine commandments). The main elaborator of Ashʿarite doctrine, al-Bāqillānī (tenth century C.E.) even recommended that belief in the atomism of time and space, that is, rejection of causality, should be "officially" required from Muslims! All this happened long before the destruction of the caliphate. It is true that Ashʿarism succeeded only gradually in establishing its hold over the Muslim world and that the support of a Sufi like al-Ghazālī (d. 1111) proved crucial for its spread and ultimate dominance as the creed of the vast majority of Sunni Islam. Nevertheless, it is not an unfair indicator of the onset of rigidity in Islamic spiritual and intellectual life that the theological system of al-Ashʿarī's contemporary the Ḥanafī al-Māturīdī (born in Maturīd, a village near Tashkent), which held more reasonable views than Ashʿarite theology on all the issues just mentioned, was eventually drowned by Ashʿarism in medieval Islam.

There is also little doubt that a sort of affinity of spirit developed between Ashʿarism and certain more extreme forms of Sufism (like the very widespread Sufism of the thirteenth-century Ibn ʿArabī), which affirmed that there was one and only one Existence in reality, namely God, and regarded all else as illusion, shadow, or appearance. But the wild rampage of this type of Sufism in the later medieval centuries is itself proof enough whither the winds were blowing and whence. This is not to deny the refinements of spirit, or the intellectual sophisitication and originality shown by many great Sufis, and it is undoubtedly true, say from the twelfth century onward, that in the face of the barrenness of "official" Islam—law and theology—most creative minds in the Muslim world gravitated into the Sufi fold. The question, however, is: Does this Sufism, with its pantheistic matrix, bear any relationship either to the theology or the social message of the Qurʾān or, indeed, to the conduct of the Prophet himself and that of the early generations of Muslims?

Institutional Change in Medieval Islam

I said a while ago that changes continued to occur in medieval Muslim society, but that these changes were not orderly or controlled. This statement has to be elaborated more precisely. First of all, the general notion that the medieval Islamic society was completely static must be dismissed as, at the very least, misleading. Modern social scientists have "discovered" that primitive societies are characterized by "stability" but that, since they lack movement, they also lack growth and creativity (the term "stable" is a euphemism for "static" or "rigid," but many social scientists prefer it because it seemingly avoids value judgment). Gunnar Myrdal found this "discovery" illuminating in his *Asian Drama* when he analyzed the backwardness of Asian countries. But surely this formula so blandly stated is both simplistic and wrong. One must ask in what respects a society is "stable" and in what respects "changing" and, if changing, whether for better or for worse. It has been found that in primitive societies conditions are so "stable" and the hold of societies over individuals so complete that even the latter's dreams are socially engineered and tend to be predictable. A society may suffer from political instability and upheavals yet be static in its social or economic or socioeconomic life, as was more or less the case with medieval societies in both the East and the West. A society may be politically stable but may undergo rapid economic growth, as has been the case generally in Western societies in recent history. Again, a society may show political stability, economic growth, and sociomoral decline, as has also been the case generally with Western societies in still more recent history. Yet again, an indifference to wealth through so-called moral concerns or indolence may result in mass poverty, which in turn may assume the proportions of a moral problem of the first order—as is the case in economically backward countries. Conversely, an obsession with purely economic values may result in social deformities and decline that may assume the character of a crucial moral issue—as is the case now with Western nations in general and as Goldsmith warned in his poem "The Deserted Village": "Ill fares the land, to hastening ills a prey, / Where wealth accumulates but men decay!"

To return to social change in medieval Islam, a brief analysis will show that the story is complex at both the theoretical and the practical levels. In the political field, Sunni Islam continued essentially to legitimize and rationalize the actual state of affairs until the fall of the Baghdad caliphate. Even after the destruction of the caliphate, Ibn Taymiya (d. 1328), recognizing the actual state of affairs, held that one global rule was not necessary for the Muslim community; what was necessary was cooperation among Muslim rulers and the discharge of their trust to their subjects. For Ibn Taymiya, the unity of the world Muslim *community* is far more fundamental than the unity of government, which in any case he held to be a necessary means to an end and not an end in itself. This principle he upheld against the Shīʿī theologian al-Ḥillī (d. 1277), who, of course, held that rule by an infallible imām belongs to the very essence of religion. For the Shīʿa, it became increasingly difficult to theoretically justify rulership in the continued absence of an infallible imām. In practice, however, there was little difference between the Sunni and Shīʿī rulers: although the problem with the Shīʿa was much more acute than with the Sunnis, both were duty-bound, in principle, to accept the limitations on their power imposed by the Sharīʿa, while both had little theoretical justification to fall back upon. Thus we note that in this important field of public life there was little or no normative link between practice and theory, primarily owing to the dearth of the latter in the later medieval centuries of Islam.

In the still more important field of law, as I said earlier, the Islamic legal system, although in the main unsystematically linked with the Qurʾān and the Sunna, was not founded on a systematic intellectual working out of the sociomoral values of the Qurʾān. In addition, from its very beginning, the legal literature of Islam has a "bookish" smell in contradistinction to the exigencies of everyday life: it is almost a purely theoretical effort. This effort is indeed vast and displays much originality, but strictly speaking it cannot be described as law—for, since it is basically concerned with morality, much of it is not enforceable in any court except that of the human conscience. Nevertheless, as the nineteenth-century Ottoman effort in the work *Majalla* clearly shows, a system of law can very well be built on it. The efforts of some modern Muslim states to replace the Sharīʿa with purely secular law are mainly the result of intellectual defeatism.

But it is true that, already in medieval Islam, certain trends in the field of law were highly detrimental to the integrity of Islamic law itself. While taking advantage of and appealing to the principles of "social necessity" and "public interest" that the Muslim jurists themselves had enunciated for the convenience of administration—so that they would not remain hidebound by the provisions of the Sharīʿa law even when circumstances demanded otherwise—Muslim rulers at the same time freely resorted to promulgating state-made law that was neither Islamic nor yet secular. There was nothing inherently wrong with these two principles themselves, provided their actual application had been reasoned on the Sharīʿa bases. But when rulers began to feel free to promulgate their own laws, based on the principles of social necessity and public interest in the absence of any reformulation or rethinking of Islamic law, the results were disastrous for Islamic law itself. What was required but never achieved was a constant reformulation and expansion of Islamic law that would have preserved its integrity and efficacy.

As I have just said, there was much that was original and fertile in the vast literature of Islamic jurisprudence, but this was out of touch with actual legal practice. The quotation from al-Shāṭibī cited in the first section of this chapter is one instance of this fertility and originality. But there are many other instances where Muslim jurists and thinkers tried to break a new trail. ʿIzz al-Dīn Ibn ʿAbd al-Salām al-Sulamī (thirteenth century C.E.), for example, rejected the ban on interest that had been almost unanimously pronounced by Muslim lawyers, as he rejected stoning to death as punishment for adultery and roundly declared the entire traditional material on the issue to be utterly unreliable. Indeed, in all great Muslim thinkers up to and including the eighteenth-century Shāh Walīy Allāh of Delhi, there is no dearth of revolutionary statements. But orthodoxy had developed an amazing shock-absorbing capacity: all these thinkers were held in high esteem by orthodox circles as great representatives of Islam, but such statements of theirs as had some radical import were invariably dismissed as "isolated" (*shādhdh*) or idiosyncratic and were quietly buried. It took real rebels like Ibn Taymiya to make any perceptible dent in this steel wall of *ijmāʿ* (consensus).

But while steady encroachments were being made upon the Sharīʿa law, not only by the state-made law but also by the customary law of different cultural regions, the ulema, the custodians of the Sharīʿa, clung tenaciously, besides personal law, to two segments of the Sharīʿa law: the "five pillars" of Islam, that is, the profession of the faith, prayer, fasting, zakāt, and pilgrimage to Mecca, on the one hand, and to the *ḥudūd,* certain punishments specified in the Qurʾān for certain crimes like murder, adultery, and theft, on the other. I have called the first category "minimal Islam" and the second "negative or punitive Islam." Actually, there was nothing theoretical at all to link these various items together. The integral teaching of the Qurʾān and the historic struggle of the Prophet that provided the sociomoral context for these provisions and institutes and cemented them together had already been lost sight of. To medieval Muslim education, then, we must now turn briefly: what was taught, how and why, and what was the end product of this educational system and its main strengths and failures.

Education in Medieval Islam

Although the beginnings of Islamic education—which meant learning the Qurʾān and developing a system of piety around it—go back in some form to the Prophet's time, it was later in the first and second centuries of Islam that scattered centers of learning grew up around persons of eminence. These teachers would normally give a student a certificate or a permit (*ijāza*) to teach what he had been taught—which in most cases consisted exclusively of memorizing the Qurʾān, copying down traditions from the Prophet and his Companions, and deducing legal points from them. Organized schools with established curricula were probably first set up by the Shīʿa to impart knowledge and indoctrinate students. When the Seljukids and Ayyubids replaced the Shīʿa states in Iran and in Egypt, large madrasas or colleges organized on Sunni lines were established, and with time they multiplied. With the establishment of the Shīʿī Safavid dynasty in Iran in the sixteenth century, there grew up a number of Twelver Shīʿa seats of higher learning, the most prominent of which at present is Qum. In Sunni Islam the position of absolute prominence is held by al-Azhar of Egypt, founded in the tenth century by the Ismāʿīlī Fatimids of Egypt and turned over to Sunni Islam after the Ayyubid conquest of Egypt in the late twelfth century. What will interest us primarily in the following account is the nature and quality of this learning and the kind of man it aimed at producing for the service of Islam.[4]

I have outlined above the rise, growth, and character of Islamic law and theology. The first to develop was law, to meet obvious administrative and judicial needs, and this was followed by theology. Islamic law, as I indicated above, is not strictly speaking law, since much of it embodies moral and quasi-moral precepts not enforceable in any court. Further, Islamic law, though a certain part of it came to be enforced almost uniformly throughout the Muslim world (and it is primarily this that bestowed homogeneity upon the entire Muslim world), is on closer examination a body of legal opinions or, as Santillana put it, "an endless discussion on the duties of a Muslim" rather than a neatly formulated code or codes. In theory, therefore, this body, even though it became rigid and inflexible as actually applied, presents a bewildering richness of legal opinions and hence a great range and flexibility in the interpretation and actual formulation of the Sacred Law (the Sharīᶜa). In other words, a system of law or even a variety of legal systems can be created on the basis of this body of opinions, even though these opinions themselves do not strictly speaking constitute law.

Law and theology formed the central part of the higher educational system of Islam imparted in the madrasas. The bare bones of Sunni theology as formulated by al-Ashᶜarī and his followers were further elaborated into systems by Fakhr al-Dīn al-Rāzī (d. 1209), al-Ījī (d. 1355), and others by incorporating certain philosophical themes like essence and existence, causation, the nature of God's attributes, and prophethood, while at the same time refuting the theses of Muslim philosphers lke Ibn Sīnā and substituting for them the countertheses of *kalām*. Similarly, the historically less important, although more reasonable, theses of the Sunni kalām system founded by al-Māturīdī were elaborated further by writers like al-Nasafī (d. 1310) and his commentator al-Taftāzānī (d. 1389). By contrast, a great revolution had occurred in Shīᶜī theology during the tenth to eleventh centuries C.E. While until then Shīᶜī kalām had been rather crude

4. For the number and size of the most important among these madrasas, their organization, finances, and number of teachers and students, the reader is referred to the more factual and analytical accounts contained in the works of various participants in the University of Chicago's recent project "Islam and Social Change," works devoted to different Muslim countries.

and anthropomorphic, an apparently sudden and remarkable change took place whereby the Shīʿa incorporated (possibly in opposition to Sunni kalām) the central Muʿtazilite doctrine of the freedom of the human will and a general emphasis on reason (although they did not accept the Muʿtazilite doctrine that good and evil are discernible by human reason, postulating instead an infallible imām as the source of sure knowledge). These skeletons of the eleventh-century Shīʿī kalām were further developed in the work of the famous Shīʿī philosopher and theologian Naṣīr al-Dīn al-Ṭūsī (d. 1274) and particularly by his brilliant disciple al-Ḥillī, not by rejecting philosophy as in the Sunni case, but by largely accepting it.[5]

Once the madrasas were organized, it was these legal and theological systems that were administered to students. We know almost nothing of what was taught in the early colleges of the twelfth, thirteenth, and fourteenth centuries. It is certain, however, that from the very beginning certain distinctions were made according to which various "sciences" or branches of learning were classified. Some of these distinctions, for example, between theoretical and practical sciences and between "universal" (*kullī*) and "particular" (*juz'ī*), sciences, were of Greek origin. By the theoretical and practical sciences was generally meant theology (also called *ʿilm al-tawḥīd*—science of the unity of God—or *uṣūl al-dīn*—principles of faith—or, later on, *ilāhiyāt*—science of theology) on the one hand, and law (called *fiqh* or, later, Sharīʿa) on the other. But when law was more systematically grounded in basic principles, these principles of law, that is, jurisprudence (*uṣūl al-fiqh*), were distinguished as a separate science from the actual law or legal rules (*ʿilm al-furūʿ*, i.e., the science of details), called *fiqh* or Sharīʿa, although both these terms continued to be used for both legal sciences.

But the most fateful distinction that came to be made in the course of time was between the "religious sciences" (*ʿulūm sharʿīya*) or "traditional sciences" (*ʿulūm naqliya*) and the "rational or secular sciences" (*ʿulūm ʿaqliya* or *ghayr sharʿīya*), toward which a gradually stiffening and stifling attitude was adopted. There are several reasons for this perilous development. First of all, the view is expressed recurrently that, since knowledge is vast while life is short, one must fix priorities; and these will naturally

5. For a more elaborate treatment of the Sunni and Shīʿī views on theology and law, see my *Islamic Methodology in History*, chap. 4.

be in favor of the religious sciences, upon whose acquisition one's success in the hereafter depends. It is extremely important to appreciate this psychological attitude, which does not reject the "rational sciences" as such but discounts them as not conducive to one's spiritual welfare. The spread of Sufism, which—in the interests of cultivating an internal spiritual life and direct religious experience—was generally inimical not only to rational sciences but to all intellectualism, is again of great importance. Despite several reminders by men like the seventeenth-century Ḥajjī Khalīfa (in his work *Mīzān al-Ḥaqq,* or *Balance of Truth*) that the Qur'ān untiringly invites men to "think," "ponder," and "reflect upon" the created universe and its extremely well-ordered and firm structure wherein no dislocations or gaps can be found, owing to the widespread opposition of the ulemā and their madrasa system to this attitude, the drift toward rejection of "rational sciences" continued. The third important reason for the gradual decline of science and philosophy was, of course, that while degree holders of religious sciences could get jobs as qadis or muftis a philosopher or a scientist was limited to court employment.

Fourth, but not least important, was the attitude of certain extraordinarily important religious personalities like al-Ghazālī. Al-Ghazālī was opposed not to science per se but to philosophy as expounded by the great Muslim philosophers like al-Fārābī and particularly Ibn Sīnā. Because of certain of their highly unorthodox metaphysical views such as the eternity of the world, the purely symbolic nature of the prophetic revelation, and the rejection of physical resurrection, al-Ghazālī and other orthodox thinkers denounced these philosophers as gravely heretical. Al-Ghazālī also asserts, rightly, that metaphysical speculation does not possess the certainty or demonstrative force of mathematical propositions. But he goes on to say, wrongly, that since the philosophy of these men is harmful to faith so must their scientific works also be shunned—since the latter tend to create goodwill in the students toward the philosophers (who were, of course, scientists too) and predisposes them to accept their philosophy! In his work *Mīzān al-ʿAmal* (*Criterion of Actions*), al-Ghazālī also invokes the argument from priorities and inveighs against those doctors who want to give priority to the medical sciences over the religious and mislead the simpleminded public by clichés such as "look after your health first and then your faith" ("*bad-*

anaka thumma dīnaka"). How could the body assume priority over the soul?

In general, primary education (given in the *maktab*s or *kuttāb*s, where reading and writing, reading of the Qur'ān, prayers, and rudimentary arithmetic were taught) was a self-contained unit and did not feed into the higher educational system. Certain official colleges, particularly those founded by the Ottoman rulers, seem to have been fully graded. For example, the educational institution established by Mehmet Fātih (the Conqueror) on both sides of the mosque he built after the conquest of Istanbul is said to have "comprised sixteen schools." Now these sixteen schools were actually sixteen grades, beginning with the elementary and ending in some sort of specialization at the advanced level. The college (or university?) of Mehmet Fātih had at its apex two divisions, one relating to "religious sciences" and the other to "rational sciences." The first division comprised theology (*ilāhiyāt*), law (*fiqh*), and literature (*adab*), while the second division had natural sciences (natural philosophy = *ṭabīʿiyāt*), philosophy (*ḥikmat*), and medicine (*ṭibb*). There were most probably no annual examinations, but students proceeded to the next higher grade at the recommendation of their teachers. So also seems to be the case with the madrasas of Sulayman the Magnificent. Again, we know little about the historical evolution of these institutions.

Astronomy, mathematics, and philosophy were also taught in medieval Iranian educational systems, along with Islamic law and theology. But in Iran, although there was government aid for madrasas (the Safavids particularly cultivated a good relationship with the ulema), the madrasas were autonomous private organizations (*ḥawza-yi ʿilmiya,* or "precincts of knowledge"). After the twelfth and thirteenth centuries, the high-level and creative philosophical tradition persisted only in Iran, where it has remained unbroken till the present. In Turkey and in the Indo-Pakistan subcontinent, however, though it continued to exist down to the modern period, its level, with few exceptions, was not high. Even in Iran, where, after the installation of Shīʿism as the state creed, philosophy continued to flourish astonishingly well, the larger body of the Shīʿī orthodox ulema have looked upon it with suspicion. That is to say, philosophy and real orthodox thought have seldom intersected each other, and though philosophers like Muḥammad Bāqir Mīr Dāmād and Mullā

Ṣadrā (both of the sixteenth to seventeenth centuries) have written on religion, their religious works seldom have been read for the sake of or have inspired orthodox thought.

In the Arab world it appears that philosophy, and probably science as well, was stricken from the curriculum as being "nonreligious," while from the fourteenth century onward the peculiarly Arab science of rhetoric and eloquence established itself as, besides theology, the major intellectual field among orthodox scholars. This science of rhetoric and eloquence was engendered in the early centuries of Islam by the Muʿtazilite interest in the linguistic "miraculousness" (*iʿjāz*) of the Qurʾān and subsequently became an independent branch of learning, one having little to do with the Greek science of rhetoric but based instead upon Arabic grammar. One reveled in appreciating rhetorical and grammatical points and niceties in an oration, a ḥadīth, or a verse of the Qurʾān. In the Qurʾān commentary of the Egyptian Shihāb al-Dīn al-Khaffājī (d. 1659), for example, a good part of the first volume is directed to the grammatical analysis of the Qurʾānic verse that appears at the beginnning of each sura of the Qurʾān and that Muslims recite before any work or undertaking, namely, "In the name of God, the Merciful, the Benevolent"! Indeed, a large part of the Qurʾān commentary literature in later medieval Islam is purely grammatical. The celebrated commentary of the Qurʾān by al-Bayḍāwī (d. ca. 1286), used so frequently in madrasas to teach the Qurʾān, is just such a work.

And so it came to pass that a vibrant and revolutionary religious document like the Qurʾān was buried under the debris of grammar and rhetoric. Ironically, the Qurʾān was never taught by itself, most probably through the fear that a meaningful study of the Qurʾān by itself might upset the status quo, not only eudcational and theological, but social as well. So one needed extrinsic props to understand the Qurʾān—and what prop could be more delicious and even intoxicating than the science of rhetoric and eloquence? It appears that at al-Azhar in these later medieval centuries this science took the place of philosophy and science and, along with theology (which included logic as an "instrumental" science) and law, constituted the essence of higher learning. As has been shown in a recently published work,[6] there was a revival of certain "secular" sciences at al-Azhar during the

6. Peter Gran, *Islamic Roots of Capitalism: Egypt 1760–1840* (Austin: University of Texas Press, 1979).

eighteenth and nineteenth centuries that preceded the modernization attempts in Egypt. In India, which remained for the most part at the periphery of Islamic intellectual developments, virtually no scientific studies developed. The eighteenth-century scholar al-Tahānavī tells us in the introduction to his famous *Kashshāf Iṣṭilāḥāt al-Funūn* (*Dictionary of Technical Terms*) that he could not find a single place in India where he could study science, and therefore in compiling the *Dictionary* he had to rely on books.

A major development that adversely affected the quality of learning in the later medieval centuries of Islam was the replacement of the original texts of theology, philosophy, jurisprudence, and such, as materials for higher instruction with commentaries and supercommentaries. The process of studying commentaries resulted in the preoccupation with hair-splitting detail to the exclusion of the basic problems of a subject. Disputation (*jadal*) became the most fashionable procedure of "winning a point" and almost a substitute for a genuine intellectual effort at raising and grappling with real issues in a field. In the earlier stages a commentary on a work was the result of a teacher's teaching that work in a class: his comments would be written down by students and then compiled into a commentary with the teacher's approval. Later, certain eminent scholars would write a condensed tract in a certain field (for example, the *Kitāb al-Tajrīd* of Naṣīr al-Dīn al-Ṭūsī on theology) or a work in verse (like the *Alfiya* of Ibn Mālik on Arabic grammar, comprising one thousand verses), so that the student might find it easier to study it or memorize it. This resulted, on the one hand, in the unfortunate habit of learning materials by rote without any deeper understanding and, on the other, in a proliferation of commentaries and supercommentaries, compounded refutations and counterrefutations. This fruitless ingenuity and waste of valuable intellectual energies culminated in such works as the Qurʾānic commentary of Fayẓī, an eminent sixteenth-century man of letters and courtier of the Mogul ruler Akbar, wherein the author dispensed with the Arabic letters of the alphabet having diacritical marks, thus reducing the number of letters he could use from twenty-eight to only thirteen. There are works written by certain Turkish scholars where, by reading words horizontally or vertically or in some cases diagonally, in each case successively or alternately (or by reading *lines* and not words alternately) on each page, one simultaneously obtains readable texts of as many as five disciplines (say, grammar, theology, law, logic, and philosophy) and in as many as three languages—Arabic, Turkish (Ottoman), and Persian! Although the presence of a large common Arabic technical vocabulary greatly facilitates the task, such works undoubtedly represent incredible feats of mental gymnastics. Finally, this development was paralleled by another type of condensed text that was not written to ease the work of students but, on the contrary, was designed to be difficult, quite like a puzzle (although it often had the merit of being easily memorizable). Commentary upon commentary was then essayed to interpret it, like al-Khayālī's (d. 1457) commentary on al-Taftāzānī's commentary on al-Nasafī. Al-Khayālī's work was so difficult that, after a series of unsuccessful commentaries upon him, the successful commentary was considered to be that of the sixteenth/seventeenth-century Indian scholar ʿAbd al-Ḥakīm (called al-Lāhūrī by later Arab authors).

With the habit of writing commentaries for their own sake and the steady dwindling of original thought, the Muslim world witnessed the rise of a type of scholar who was truly encyclopedic in the scope of his learning but had little new to say on anything. This category of scholar-cum-commentator must be distinguished on the one hand from a very different type of a comprehensive thinker like Aristotle or even a lesser figure like Ibn Sīnā, who welded a variety of fields of inquiry into a unified system and coherent world view, and on the other hand from the modern type of specialist whose knowledge has extremely narrow confines. The latter-day medieval Muslim scholar I am talking about "studied" all the fields of knowledge available, but he did this mainly through commentaries and was himself a commentator and a compiler. This type of scholar is, of course, not confined to the Muslim world but is also representative of many medieval European savants. One important but implicit assumption of this type is that scholarship is not regarded as an active pursuit, a creative "reaching out" of the mind to the unknown—as is the case today—but rather as the more or less passive acquisition of already established knowledge. This attitude naturally is not conducive to original inquiry and thought, since it assumes that all that can be known about reality is already known except, perhaps, for a few "gaps" to be filled by interpretation and extension or some angularities to be smoothed out. The view that mind is creative in knowledge is essentially a characterisitc of modern theories of knowledge.

Islamic mysticism produced its own theory of knowledge, holding that what is learned from books does not constitute knowledge at all; knowledge is that which is vouchsafed to a Sufi by God in a direct intuitive experience. Sufis rejected both learning and intellectual thought as positively harmful. This Sufi experience was characterized by immediacy and certainty that rendered it immune from falsehood and secure from doubt. Although a number of important post-twelfth-century philosophers, such as al-Suhrawardī (d. 1191), Ṣadr al-Dīn al-Shīrāzī (Mullā Ṣadrā, d. 1641), and others, advocated and claimed for themselves the ability to combine rationality with intuitive experience, Sufis as such poured contempt on rationality. In their *zāwiya*s or *khānqāh*s the Sufis, besides performing their spiritual exercises and providing guidance for their disciples, also taught important works of Sufi spirituality like the *Mathnavī* of Jalāl al-Dīn al-Rūmī (d. 1273). When later the gap between the ulema and the Sufis became narrower and many of the ulema themselves enrolled in the more orthodox Sufi orders, it was not uncommon for a khānqāh to impart both a madrasa type of orthodox education and Sufi spiritual works, for which, indeed, the most popular Sufi figure of eleventh-century Baghdad, ʿAbd al-Qādir al-Jīlānī, had already set an example.

Islamic Education in the Indo-Pakistan Subcontinent

I stated earlier that education in Indian Islam was generally not of a very high order. This must be elaborated and made more specific. The fact is that when organized education got under way in India in the thirteenth and fourteenth centuries the formative and creative stages of various sciences in Islam had already essentially passed, and these sciences were in fact either static or in decline. Outside India at that time, commentaries and encyclopedic learning held sway. It was these later texts and their commentaries, therefore, that came to form the content of Islamic education in India. The first sciences to be introduced were law and theology. In the fifteenth century, logic begins to receive more emphasis, as does the "science of rhetoric and eloquence," and philosophy gains prominence during the

Mogul period, particularly during the reign of Akbar. At about the same time (early seventeenth century), Ḥadīth receives its first major impulse, thanks to the writings of ʿAbd al-Ḥaqq of Delhi, called "the Muḥaddith." In the eighteenth century, the famous "Niẓāmī" curriculum (*Dars-i-Niẓāmī*) was issued by Mullā Niẓām al-Dīn (d. 1747) of the Firangī Maḥal madrasa in Lucknow. This was a nine- or ten-year syllabus of middle to higher education including sixteen different subjects and eighty-three works in all. The subjects (as has since become the common practice in most madrasas) progressed in the following manner: Arabic grammar (twelve works); rhetoric (three); prosody (one); logic (ten); philosophy (four); Arabic literature—prose and poetry (seven); theology (five); history of Islam (three); medicine—including the part "On Fevers" of Ibn Sīnā's *Qānūn* (four); astronomy (two); geometry (one—twenty chapters of Euclid); art of disputation (one); law (eight); jurisprudence (six); law of inheritance (one); principles of Ḥadīth (one); Ḥadīth (ten); principles of Qurʾān—interpretation (one); Qurʾān—commentaries (four).[7]

For instruction in principles of Qurʾān—interpretation (*uṣūl al-tafsīr*), Aḥmad's list gives *al-Fawz al-Kabīr fī uṣūl al-Tafsīr* by Shāh Walīy Allāh of Delhi (d. 1762). Since Niẓām al-Dīn returned to Delhi from his education in Medina about 1732 and died in 1747, either this work was written between these two dates or it was inserted into the syllabus after Niẓām al-Dīn's death, which may well be the case, since there are other works in the list that are definitely later insertions.

This means that the syllabus began to be modified soon after its compilation; the trend has been toward simplification and the elimination of several works and even of whole fields, like science and philosophy. Walīy Allāh himself wrote a much more simplified syllabus in which, although some of the physical sciences were kept, their importance was reduced. However, he strongly recommended that the Qurʾān should be studied by itself without any commentary, if possible, and that the commentaries used should be brief ones that clarify grammatical constructions or meanings of words or give the historical background of the verses.

7. Nadhr Aḥmad, *Jāʾizah-yi Madāris-i ʿArabiyyah Islamiyyah Maghribi Pakistān* [A survey of Arabic madrasas of West Pakistan] (Lahore: Muslim Academy, 1972), pp. 587 ff.

While the syllabus of Niẓam al-Dīn is weighted toward "rational sciences," that of Shāh Walīy Allāh is weighted toward the core traditional sciences of Islam—law, theology, and Ḥadīth—with the innovation that he formally includes works of Sufism at the end of the syllabus—a novel feature in the orthodox educational system. These two syllabi form the basis of practically all madrasa syllabi until today, with various combinations and modifications suiting the temper and orientation of a given institution, its founder, and its faculty. The general trend, undoubtedly under the impact of the profound fundamentalist influence of Walīy Allāh's school of thought, has been to eliminate the intellectual and rational sciences and emphasize the purely "religious" orthodox disciplines. The wide propagation of Ḥadīth in the subcontinent is definitely due to the massive influence of Shāh Walīy Allāh and his sons and students. The Deoband seminary in northern India (U.P.) was established in the latter half of the nineteenth century by scholars descended from the school of Shāh Walīy Allāh.

Since, however, Walīy Allāh's school not only represented an educational institution like Niẓām al-Dīn's Firangī Maḥal but was essentially a puritanical reformist endeavor, this latter orientation, in its impact, proved a watershed. On the one hand, its mainstream came to be represented by institutions like the Deoband seminary (although Deoband proved to be much less broad and interpretive than Walīy Allāh himself); on the other, it resulted in the rise of the Ahl-i-Ḥadīth school, which tended to be a right-wing extreme, emphasizing Ḥadīth to the exclusion not only of purely rational sciences like philosophy but even of kalām theology, of whose validity it was, like the mainstream of the Hanbalites, very suspicious. But the purist ideas of the school of Walīy Allāh also created a strong reaction in the form of the nineteenth-century Barelavī school of thought, which was a conscious reassertion, in the face of Deoband and the Ahl-i-Ḥadīth, of the mass religion, with strong overtones of popular Sufi beliefs in the powers of saints and mythification of the person of the Prophet Muḥammad. It took its name from the town of Barelī, whence hailed its most vocal representative, Muḥammad Riẓā, who waged lengthy disputations with his opponents on such questions as whether the Prophet Muḥammad was all-knowing (*ʾilm al ghaib* = the unseen), whether he had a body of light, and so forth. Whereas politically Deoband and Ahl-i-Ḥadīth were in general patently anti-British, representatives of the Barelavī school issued authoritative statements (*fatwās*) in favor of British rule.

In Pakistan, then, besides the Shīʿī madrasas, there have survived three types of traditional Sunni madrasas: the Deobandī, the Ahl-i-Ḥadīth, and the Barelavī. While at the time of partition Pakistan had only 137 madrasas, the number rose to 210 in 1950, 401 in 1960, and 563 in 1971; the total number of big and small madrasas is said to be at least 893, with a total of 3,186 teachers and 32,384 regular students.[8] The rapid increase in the number of madrasas since the establishment of Pakistan is striking. The basic reason for this increase is no doubt that the state of Pakistan was established on the basis of Islam. It is interesting that increase in the number of madrasas and in knowledge about traditional orthodox Islam appears to have been much more marked in smaller towns and in the countryside (in some areas of the Punjab it has been spectacular) than in the cities, where Karachi and Lahore have also seen expansion in madrasas. Whereas in the cities traditional Islam progressively yields to industry and secular education, resulting in modern interpretations of Islam or secularism, traditional orthodox Islam has gained immense ground in smaller towns. I shall try to trace this whole development in the next two chapters.

8. Ibid., pp. 688 ff.

2

Classical Islamic Modernism and Education

Introduction

We saw in chapter 1 that a kind of secularism appeared in the Muslim world in premodernist times because of the stagnation of Islamic thinking in general and, more particularly, because of the failure of Sharīʿa law and institutions to develop themselves to meet the changing needs of the society. This affected the course of modern Islam, particularly in the field of education, as we shall see in this chapter. There are, however, substantial differences in the character of modern developments in different Muslim regions, which are perhaps mainly to be accounted for by four factors: (1) whether a particular cultural region retained its sovereignty vis-à-vis the European political expansion and whether it was dominated and governed de jure or de facto by a European colonial power; (2) the character of the organization of the ulema, or religious leadership, and the character of their relationship with the governing institutions before the colonial encroachment; (3) the state of the development of Islamic education and its accompanying culture immediately before the colonial encroachment; and (4) the character of the overall colonial policy of the particular colonizing power—British, French, or Dutch.

Thus, among those important Muslim countries that came under Western influence, Turkey alone managed to keep her independence from direct or indirect rule (although not from all sorts of Western pressures and interventions), while Arabia, for example, though a religiously (and hence politically) important Muslim country, did not experience any Western impact. Again, while India came under direct British rule for a long period and while North Africa came under French rule and Indonesia under Dutch, Egypt and Iran came under such Western hegemonic pressures that, even though their rulers were generally not as powerless or titular as, for example, those of Nigeria, their policies were not independent. Again, whereas both the British and the Dutch colonial policies allowed the cultures and educational systems of the countries they ruled to remain and to develop more or less freely, the French policy of "assimilation" tried to implant French culture and education not by the side of native culture and education, but at their expense and, indeed, in Algeria, at the cost of their almost total annihilation. The French also encouraged the Sufi orders in North Africa over the orthodox Islam of the ulema, which they feared, whereas the British and the Dutch, on the whole, did not do this; their policies, if anything, were more conducive to the growth of orthodox Islam. I shall also have to leave out of this study the central Asian Islamic lands, where all religious education, and indeed life, was blighted by the Soviet communist regime; although Islam has seen some revival there lately (together with an underground resistance movement, mainly Sufi), proper information is lacking.

This much for factors 1 and 4 enumerated above by way of introduction—their elaboration will come presently when I treat different regions of the Muslim world in greater detail. Factor 2 concerns the nature of the organization of the ulema and their relationship with the political authority in precolonial days. Here again we see great differences. Whereas, for example, the ulema were highly organized in Egypt (where they were practically concentrated at al-Azhar) and in Turkey, they were quite scattered in India (although they were nevertheless always a powerful element in the state as well) and in Indonesia. In Iran, although the ulema enjoyed greater influence over state policies than their Sunni counterparts, except in Turkey, they were gathered in madrasas at certain main centers but had no overall organization. Furthermore, while in Turkey the ulema represented a powerful class of the governing authority—almost like a Christian *ecclesia* (the term *ʿālim* in the Ottoman empire did not mean only a "scholar" or a "religious scholar," as it normally did in the Muslim world, but designated an *official* status)—in Egypt there was no such quasi-ecclesiastic service beyond that of the government judges that existed throughout the Muslim world, and indeed in India and Indonesia they hardly had any aura of official power.

As for the state of development of the medieval Islamic educational system before the impact of the West, we recall from the preceding chapter that the later medieval centuries saw a marked decline—indeed a stagnation—of intellectual life in the Muslim world. From the thirteenth/fourteenth centuries onward there was an era of manuals, commentaries, and supercommentaries. That a great deal of ingenuity lies buried in these generally ponderous and repetitive works, and that in Iran there was much originality in philosophy, is indubitable, but in an overall review this literature is singularly unoriginal, pedantic, and superficial. Still, the most highly developed countries in terms of sophistication, if not originality, were Turkey and Egypt, mainly because the traditional education in these countries was highly organized and concentrated. Since state Shīʿism set Iran apart from the rest of the Muslim world, that country became basically isolated and developed a spiritualized intellectualism known as *ʿirfān,* or "Islamic gnosis," which although it did make some impact on India is almost peculiar to Iran from the sixteenth through the nineteenth centuries. Behind Turkey, Egypt, and Iran came India, with some of its most brilliant commentaries and a few original thinkers like the eighteenth-century Shāh Walīy Allāh of Delhi and his nineteenth-century school. What is now Pakistan could boast of the internationally known commentator-intellectual of the seventeenth century, ʿAbd al-Ḥakīm of Sialkot (called al-Lāhūrī by the Arabs), but besides that it possessed little by way of first-rate intellectual productivity and much more of Sufi orders. Indeed, in the countryside of Pakistan—and even in many of its towns—orthodox learning did not become widespread until after 1947. Perhaps this premodernist relative intellectual poverty in Pakistan largely explains its current situation in the field of general intellectual development, both religious and nonreligious.

In Indonesia, orthodox learning at a high level was hardly cultivated before the beginning of the twentieth century. Beginning with the year 1900, certain Indonesians who had gone to

Mecca and spent years there cultivating orthodox Islamic intellectualism—notably orthodox theology and Ḥadiīth—began spreading their learning in the Indonesian *pesantrens,* which gradually developed into madrasas. In the 1930s the influence of Cairo's al-Azhar assumed a certain dominance in Indonesian Islam. It is highly interesting and significant, as we shall see in greater detail later, that those Indonesian ulema who were trained in Cairo became members of the more progressive and modernist Muḥammadiya organization, while those coming from Mecca enrolled largely in the conservative and more typically Javanese Nahḍat al-ʿUlamāʾ, which was nearer to the folk Islam of Java than was the former.

Yet, important though these local and regional differences are in the development of the Muslim responses to modernizing changes in the field of education—and it will be a major concern of mine to bring these differences out—the underlying uniformity of these responses must not be lost sight of. Despite stimuli of various degrees of directness and intensity, the responses were basically conditioned by the nature of the medieval intellectual temper of Islam, which, thanks to the amazing uniformity of the madrasa education, was equally amazingly uniform. Before coming to portray the regional developments *in practice* in Islamic educational modernism, therefore, I will try to analyze the theoretical bases of this practical response. These theoretical bases themselves show a development throughout the nineteenth and twentieth centuries, with different strands of the modernist argument sometimes going on simultaneously, sometimes succeeding one another, but always *functionally* related to the élan and justification of change.

Theoretical Considerations

Two basic approaches to modern knowledge have been adopted by modern Muslim theorists: (1) that the acquisition of modern knowledge be limited to the practical technological sphere, since at the level of pure thought Muslims do not need Western intellectual products—indeed, that these should be avoided, since they might create doubt and disruption in the Muslim mind, for which the traditional Islamic system of belief already provides satisfactory answers to ultimate questions of world view; and (2) that Muslims without fear can and ought to acquire not only Western technology but also its intellectualism, since no type of knowledge can be harmful, and that in any case science and pure thought were assiduously cultivated by Muslims in the early medieval centuries, whence they were taken over by Europeans themselves. To be sure, there are various nuances of these views and also "middle-term" positions—for example, that, besides technology, pure science is also good but not the pure thought of the modern West, or the more recent view that technology may even be harmful without adequate ethical training—but the two approaches set out here provide a good starting point for the modernist discussion of education.

It is obvious that the first view is conducive to a dualistic attitude and will eventually result in a "secularist" state of mind, that is, a duality of loyalty to religion and to "worldly affairs." This first approach was considered the patently correct answer to the problem of the modernization of education in the early phase of Turkish modernism, in which modern education was identified with "useful skills" and "practical knowledge." The chief reason for this official attitude was, of course, that the ulema, the official class of religious leaders, was against the modernizing of the Muslim mind through education: acquiring practical skills, that is, professional knowledge (engineering, medicine, etc.) called *fann,* p. *funūn,* was all right provided the traditional madrasa education was left free to impart *ʿilm,* that is, the Sharīʿa knowledge for the cultivation of the Muslim mind and spirit. To the Turkish reformers in general, this dualism represented the dualism of the eternal and the changing, which were identified respectively with religion (the other worldly) and mundane life (the this-worldly). For many modernists this may have been primarily a question of *strategy* to minimize the offense to the ulema, but that the ulema as a whole should have regarded it as inoffensive seems strange to us now, for in the sphere of "this world" lies the whole gamut not only of "skills" but of social life, with its institutions and laws in which the Sharīʿa claimed to operate. But neither the modernist nor the ulema at this stage clearly saw the implications of educational modernization in terms of "skills" for social life and its values.

This "practical" bent is clearly brought out in the educational reforms of the era of Mahmud II that led to the mentality of the Tanẓīmāt leaders. While education could not be touched by the modernists, nor the higher madrasa education, the emphasis fell on the creation of higher professional education, engineering, medicine, and so forth. On primary education, Mahmud's decree of 1824 clearly states that a knowledge of the requisites of religion is incumbent upon all Muslims and must take precedence over all "worldly" considerations, wherefore *no* parent shall henceforth prevent his child from attending a school where he shall learn the Qurʾān and articles of faith.[1] Yet, the Board of Useful Affairs created by Mahmud's own reorganized government issued a report in 1838 that stated:

> All arts and trades are products of science. Religious knowledge serves salvation in the world to come but science serves perfection of man in this world. Astronomy, for example, serves the progress of navigation and the development of commerce. The mathematical sciences lead to the orderly conduct of warfare. . . . Innumerable new and useful inventions, like the use of steam, came into existence in this manner. . . . Without science, the people cannot know the meaning of love for the state and fatherland. . . . The Ottoman Commonwealth *had* schools and scholars (i.e., scientists), but they disappeared. Later, military, naval, engineering and medical schools were opened with great effort, but students entering these schools lacked even ordinary knowledge for the proper reading of Turkish books. This was because of the defectiveness of the primary schools.[2]

Since the infrastructure for these higher "secular" professional schools was not forthcoming from the traditional primary schools, certain new secondary (*rüshdiye*) schools were opened under the Tanzīmāt reformers. Under Tanzīmāt leadership, the gulf between the traditional and the modern widened systematically and immeasurably in all fields, not least in education. The Tanzīmāt leaders, who did drink heavily, and for the most part one-sidedly, at the gushing fountains of Western—particularly French—thought, were basically secularized men who lacked even the courage to face up to the issue of reforming traditional education. It was much easier to juxtapose the modern and the traditional. This meant the new "enlightenment" for the few but the same old rut for the large masses of the

1. Niyazi Berkes, *The Development of Secularism in Turkey,* (Montreal: McGill University Press, 1964), pp. 100–101.
2. Ibid., p. 105.

people. The gulf between the traditional and the modern, the "other worldly and eternal" and the "this-worldly and transitory," came to be the gulf between the elite and the Turkish masses. And since the Tanzīmātists were professional followers and appeasers of the Western powers and their protégé Christian minorities within the Ottoman rule, their overly pro-Western stand provoked a severe reaction among the Young Ottomans—particularly Ziya Paša and Namik Kemāl—who regarded the Tanzīmāt movement as both anti-Islamic and anti-Turkish. These Young Ottomans therefore stressed, besides modernization, Islamic and national elements in education. Ziya Paša wrote:

> Is there not a difference of climate?
> Is the situation of East and West the same?
> Could Racine or Lamartine adorn a Kasida like Nefi?
> Could Senai or Farazdak write plays like Molière?

Again:

> Islam, they say, is a stumbling block to the progress of the state;
> This story was not known before and now it is the fashion.
> Forgetting our religious loyalty in all our affairs
> Following Frankish ideas is now the fashion.[3]

The idea that modern "useful" technology may be introduced into a society while the traditional integrity of that society can be still maintained is, of course, naive. But with many Muslims it was and continues to be the standard response. Yet those who hold the opposite view—that technological modernization necessarily entails wholesale or nearly wholesale Westernization—are no less naive. This was, however, the stance of the majority of Tanzīmātists. But with the Young Ottomans like Ziya Paša and Namik Kemāl a new note was struck that was different from both: political, scientific, and correspondingly social modernization along with technological while the cultural integrity of the nation remains intact.

In the latter half of the nineteenth century five prominent Muslim modernists were to formulate and expound the positive attitude of Islam toward science and an unhampered investigation of nature—Sayyid Aḥmad Khān and Sayyid Amīr ʿAlī of

3. Bernard Lewis, *Emergence of Modern Turkey* (Oxford: Oxford University Press, 1961), pp. 135, 136.

India, Jamāl al-Dīn al-Afghānī, Namik Kemāl of Turkey, and Shaykh Muḥammad ʿAbduh. Amīr ʿAlī was the youngest of these; among the rest, it is difficult to say who was the earliest. Most probably Sayyid Aḥmad Khān was, since he had done some work on the reformulation of theology even before the Indian rebellion of 1857, at the insistence of some of his British friends, although his undiluted modernism begins in the 1860s after his brief stay in England. Al-Afghānī might be considered next except that his visit to Europe occurred at least a decade and a half after Sayyid Aḥmad Khān's: before this his major modernist statement on the cultivation of science was his address delivered in Istanbul in December 1870 (on the occasion of the opening of the Dār al-Funūn) which, though aroused by contemporary needs, had as its source of inspiration the medieval Muslim scientists and philosopher Ibn Sīnā (d. 1037). Since the views of Ibn Sīnā on the relationship between religion and philosophy had been severely castigated by the Islamic orthodoxy as extremely heretical, al-Afghānī's above-mentioned address caused such a furor that he had to leave Turkey. Namik Kemāl, who had stayed and studied in Europe from 1867 to 1871, comes next, and finally comes Shaykh Muḥammad ʿAbduh, who was in Europe with al-Afghānī.

All these men, who were contemporaries, enthusiastically preached the cultivation of science and appropriation of the scientific spirit of the West, although among them only Namik Kemāl had actually been a student (of law and economics) in the West. Considering that, except for al-Afghānī and ʿAbduh, these men hardly met each other, their arguments are amazingly similar. The integral constituents of their reasoning are (1) that the flowering of science and the scientific spirit from the ninth to the thirteenth century among Muslims resulted from the fulfillment of the insistent Qur'ānic requirement that man study the universe—the handiwork of God, which has been created for his benefit; (2) that in the later medieval centuries the spirit of inquiry had severely declined in the Muslim world and hence Muslim society had stagnated and deteriorated; (3) that the West had cultivated scientific studies that it had borrowed largely from Muslims and hence had prospered, even colonizing the Muslim countries themselves; and (4) that therefore Muslims, in learning science afresh from the developed West, would be both recovering their past and refulfilling the neglected commandments of the Qurʾān.

At this stage the earlier argument for "useful" technology is replaced by a demand to cultivate science as such: technology is certainly useful, but what is of primary importance is the cultivation of the spirit of scientific inquiry as demanded by the Qurʾān. If we look at the three major exponents of this doctrine—Aḥmad Khān, Namik Kemāl, and Muḥammad ʿAbduh—we see that, beyond their basic agreement on the argument outlined above, they reveal substantial differences in attitude, especially as concerns the implications of modern science for the traditional weltanschauung and for the realm of faith. In view of the fact that modern science asserts the eternity and immutability of natural law, does this science leave any room for a God who is the creator and sustainer of the universe and who will destroy it at the approach of the Day of Resurrection? What can revelation mean for modern science? Will faith radically adjust itself to these new conceptions, or must there be mutual adjustment and interaction, or must the realms of faith and science keep separate? For Muḥammad ʿAbduh, although the medieval Muslim cosmology and world view can be challenged by science, faith as such cannot; for faith, by its very nature, cannot be touched by science: the two have separate orbits and each must keep within its own. Namik Kemāl would not admit the claims of modern science beyond what is empirically proved: since no one can ever prove the immutability of natural laws, there is not the slightest reason to believe in their eternity. God has made these laws and can unmake them as well. In this sense, Kemāl is perhaps the most "orthodox" Muslim of the three, since, unlike ʿAbduh, he subordinates the claims of science to the requirements of faith. While ʿAbduh attempts to reintroduce a Muʿtazilite type of rationalism into orthodox Islam and can even defend the medieval Muslim philosophers' rejection of physical resurrection, Kemāl, although proud of the Muslim philosophers' achievements in the fields of science and philosophy, will not allow rationalism to destroy faith and has nothing but scorn for the Muʿtazila, who, despite their rationalist claims, were intolerant and illiberal.

Sayyid Aḥmad Khān is easily the most radical spirit of the three reformers. For him there is no doubt that the modern scientific spirit or the laws of nature must set the criteria for judging the acceptibility of a certain faith. So judged, Islam turns out to be, among the religions of the world, most in conformity with the laws of nature, and of all religious documents the Qurʾān is the most rational. Since Muslims have grossly misunderstood and misinterpreted the Qurʾānic world view in the past, and since the orthodox Muslim theology is no longer valid, a fresh theology must be created from the Qurʾān in the light of modern experience. In attempting this, Sayyid Aḥmad Khān utilizes the arguments not only of the Muʿtazila but, indeed patently, those of the Muslim philosophers. No wonder he turns out in the end to be almost a naturalist deist. Because his views were radical, he was not able to implement them in the Aligarh Muslim college created by him for the express purpose of integrating religious beliefs with a modern scientific outlook. In the end, as we shall see in the next section, religious education at Aligarh had to be left to traditionalist teachers who had no modern education whatever.

While at the higher educational level the modernists thus eased the adoption of modern science for the younger generation, there appeared a new type of work that brought home the practical moral content of Islam in the form of attractive stories. This was a major development, since before this the only teaching of moral duties was through "religious" books that emphasized the consequences of wrong doing not in terms of harm done to society or to the wrongdoer as part of the society, but in terms of heaven and hell. Not only did the new literature make the moral impact of conduct more intelligible to the young reader, thus making moral teaching more effective, but its anecdotal form made reading more pleasant. This was in line with the attitude of the premodernist reformers of the eighteenth and nineteenth centuries, who had conceived of superstitions and antisocial practices in terms of social and moral degeneration in this world rather than in terms of otherworldly consequences. Muslims already had a "secular" ethical literature like the *Akhlāq-i-Nāṣirī* and *Akhlāq-i-Jalālī*—books that had already been studied as part of the general Islamic literature if not of the madrasa curriculum—but this was of a philosophical character. The new literature was produced for children.

Closely allied with this trend and, to an extent, genetically related to it is the revival of interest in the past, both Islamic and local (national), historical and valuational. If the interest in modern scientism oriented the Muslims to the contemporary West, a study of their own history and value system reoriented them both toward Islam and toward their local, national traditions. It has been remarked by several students of modern Islam, including myself, that, in the rediscovery of their tradition by modern Muslims, Islamic and national elements go together. This has often been characterized as a contradiction. As the two sides developed they undoubtedly created a tension between nationalism and pan-Islamism, but while uncompromising nationalists like Muṣṭafā Kemāl and Muṣṭafā Kāmil were necessarily secular, it seems that in their genesis the two are closely allied or in fact even identified, and that the feeling for local nationalism was encouraged by identity with the Islamic past. Thus, Namik Kemāl could write both dramas, *Ṣalāḥ al-Dīn Ayyūbī* and *Vatan* (*The Fatherland*), with the same feeling and motivation. In the historical vision of Amīr ʿAlī, Shiblī, and Iqbāl, the Islamic history of Spain is indistinguishable from the Islamic history of India. Even a secular social and socialist reformer, the central Asian Ismāʿil Gasprinsky, could envision a regenerated and scientifically developed Muslim society that, in his dramatic work, he placed in Spain. To the secular Western scholars of Islam like W. Cantwell Smith this is modern Muslim "romanticism," just as to the Muslim modernist modern Western secular nationalism is "idolatry."

It is this psychological-intellectual development that resulted in demands for a system of education that would be modern but at the same time imbued with national-Islamic values, whether national is seen as part of the Islamic goal or Islamic is viewed as part of the national. The concept of a culture-oriented education was developed in its most accentuated form by the Turkish sociologist Zia Gökalp, who believed that, whereas science and the civilization founded upon it were universal and could be appropriated by any nation, culture and value commitments were unique growths peculiar to every society and its national ethos and religion was part of culture. The goal of education was to inculcate these value commitments through *tarbiya* (moral training) and communicate scientific knowledge through *taʿlīm* (education). This sharp distinction between national cultural values and scientific or universal knowledge is finally untenable; nevertheless, the assumption on which it rests, that modern science is cultivable in a variety of cultural settings, not only is not invalid but is correct, as subsequent experience has shown. Gökalp was, however, attacked by one-track Westernizers like Ismail Hakki Baltacioğlu, who patently misunderstood the meaning of Gökalp's stand, as pure traditionalism harmful to the cultivation of modernity. Baltacioğlu, in fact, advocated that cultural values be suppressed by the educational system, not encouraged by it. It is clear that Baltacioğlu understood the "cultural values" of Gökalp to be what was actually being imparted by parents to children, that is, the moral status quo of the society. In a similar vein, Ṭahā Husayn in his *Mustaqbal al-thaqāfa fī Miṣr* (*The Future of Culture in Egypt*) attempted to prove that Egypt was essentially a Western land in terms of cultural orientation. Earlier, Sayyid Aḥmad Khān had strongly advocated, through his Urdu journal *Tahdhīb-i-akhlāq,* the adoption by Indian Muslims of the entire life-style of Victorian England.

Two factors, however, already hinted at above, determined Muslim countries not to identify themselves totally with the West through adopting entirely Western curricula: national aspirations of varying degrees of intensity and Islamic values. The first country to feel the impact of national aspirations was, again, Turkey. Gökalp had already elaborated a nationalist cultural ideology of education. The main change that occurred at the hands of Muṣṭafā Kemāl and his colleagues was that religion (Islam) was ousted from the public-school curriculum. But even though a great plunge was taken to acquire Western learning, apparently at the expense of Islam, Turkish nationalism, of which the firebrand Atatürk was an embodiment, had already incorporated Islam as its integral constituent, and despite Atatürk's personal allergy to religion Islam returned to national education—via nationalism—as inevitably as day follows night. Thus, despite the potential conflict of nationalism with Islam, there is an important sense in which they are inseparable (witness the closing of the two Christian missionary schools in Bursa and Izmir by Atatürk's government following the conversion to Christianity of two Muslim girls).

In Muslim countries other than Turkey that were under direct or indirect Western colonial rule, Islam reasserted itself with a vengeance. First, as I indicated earlier, their peoples felt a much greater need to buttress their own identity away from the multiple colonial invasion—political, economic, intellectual, and moral—and hence proportionately emphasized their Islamicity.

In several cases, notably in Indonesia, they set up their own educational institutions as distinguished from the public, colonial-government sponsored schools. Alternatively, they sent their children (sons for the most part) to the "public" secular schools in the morning and to Islamic instruction centers in the afternoon or evening. Second, in all liberation movements directed against the colonial powers, the Islamic concept of jihād was heavily relied upon to arouse the sentiments of the general public against foreign rulers; so too was the Qur'ānic verse (4:59) "obey God, the Messenger [i.e., Muḥammad], and those put in authority over you *from among yourselves,*" which implies that Muslims must not obey non-Muslim rulers. In other words, those concepts of Islam that make for a strong and cohesive Muslim community came to the fore.

But in the meantime other developments—quite apart from nationalism—took place that demanded a much weightier and more basic share for Islam in the newly emerging educational systems. Among those nations that were contiguous with or very close to Europe, particularly Turkey, there was already present in the latter half of the nineteenth century a realization that something was direly morally wrong with the West. Colonialism and economic imperialism were obvious evils; that is, exploitation of the resources of politically and industrially weaker nations to enrich "homelands" (of which Rome had been the first though limited example, but of which Western Europe became the full-scale embodiment, particularly in the nineteenth century). These nations were mortal enemies of each other and they were brutal exploiters of dominated nations, although each of them was at home a democracy with an increasingly liberal, tolerant, and humanitarian outlook. Those Muslims who visited these Western countries were struck by this double, or rather multiple, standard of these beacons of civilization. But since international politics adhered to the law of the jungle, they had no choice but to play by the rules; in fact, many of them borrowed this type of "nationalism" for their own countries as well.

Sayyid Aḥmad Khān, as I hinted earlier, had developed a reformist ideology of Islam at whose center was the creation of a new "science of theology" that would not only be compatible with the weltanschauung born of the new nineteenth-century scientism—as Muḥammad ʿAbduh held—but would grow out of this weltanschauung and the Qur'ānic teaching at the same time.

He was convinced that the latter absolutely backed the former. As I indicated before, his dream did not come true, at least not in his lifetime, for while he imported most of Aligarh's modern science teachers from Europe, particularly England, community pressure forced him to leave the teaching of religion to gentlemen brought from Deoband. The first generation produced from Aligarh naturally scoffed at the teachers of the Deobandi Islam, whom they regarded as survivals from the medieval past. Since, however, these early specimens of the Aligarh crop were not very well grounded in Western sciences—for it needed time to produce scholars who could even understand well the spirit of the new intellectual culture, let alone compete with their Western intellectual fathers in their own fields—they naturally invited the ridicule of the representatives of the older and more mature Islamic culture.

So disquieted was Muḥammad Shiblī Nuʿmānī, the Indian historian of Islam and of Persian literature, with what he regarded as the extreme Westernism of the early crop of Aligarh that he developed a new educational ideology that, to acquaint Muslim youth with Islamic culture, placed a greater emphasis on secular Arabic literature. He pioneered a new educational institution, called the Nadwat al-ʿUlamāʾ (the Assembly of the Ulema) at Lucknow, of which I shall speak in the next section. A particularly prominent feature of the Nadwa education was the study of history, not so much to inculcate a truly historical spirit as to develop self-confidence and pride in the achievements of the Muslim past.

Iqbāl wrote no philosophy of education, let alone a program for the education of Muslims. Yet what he expressed by way of impatience with the existing forms of education—the orthodox, the Sufi, and the modern—was extremely powerful. Positive Sufism, the inculcation of a dynamic personality in service of truth, he appreciated deeply; but that was gone, and a negative Sufism, an escape from the problems of the world, was all that remained. In its growing influence upon the ulema it had also destroyed the dynamism of the orthodox. Further, the orthodox had little left with them beyond meaningless philological discussions and hair-splitting details of questions more or less irrelevant to life. Of course, Iqbāl was looking for an educational system that would render the human personality not just "informed" but creative and dynamic. Of the orthodox ʿālim and the Sufi adept he wrote:

> I have a complaint O God! against the schoolmen:
> They are training the children of falcons to roll in dust.

Again:

> You have been throttled at the outset by schoolmen,
> Whence shall come the cry "There is no God but Allah"?[4]

Iqbāl was a particularly severe critic of modern knowledge, which seemed to him almost wholly weighted toward technology and materialism and destructive of higher human values. In his poem *Pīr-i-Rūmī wa Murīd-i-Hindī,* where he questions Rūmī on important issues and selects appropriate answers from Rūmī's *Mathnavī,* the opening verse is:

> The seeing eye sheds tears of blood;
> Modern knowledge has become destructive of religion,

to which Rūmī answers:

> If you apply knowledge [only] to your body, it is like a poisonous snake.
> If you apply it to your heart, it becomes your friend.

But in the same poem Iqbāl complains also of the depersonalizing effects that British education was having on Indian Muslims in particular:

> Alas! the young and hot-blooded schoolboy
> Is falling a helpless victim to the Western sorcerer,

to which Rūmī replies:

> A bird caged for long, when it tries to fly,
> Becomes an easy victim for every rending cat.[5]

This verse is a critique of both the traditional and the modern educational systems, the one incarcerating the mind and spirit in a cage, the second not merely giving a materialistic education that was out of tune with higher human values and particularly with the spiritual culture of Islam, but indoctrinating Muslim

4. Muḥammad Iqbāl, *Bāl-i-Jibrīl* (Lahore, Shaikh Ghulām ʾAlī, 1962), pp. 50, 69.
5. Ibid., p. 180 ff.

youth with the superiority of Western culture. It was the creation of *men* that, for Iqbāl, was the goal of education. Traditional Muslim education had with rare exceptions failed in this for centuries; perhaps its greatest trouble was that it had created the same dualism between the religious and the secular, between this-worldly and that-worldly, from which Christianity, for example, had suffered from its very beginnings. The "religious" scholar had become a "professional" in his own field, but he was ignorant of and unable to cope with the problems of the world he lived in. Now the test of true spirituality or religious life is that it should solve these problems creatively; otherwise its claims to being spiritual or religious are untenable. And so Iqbāl asks Rūmī:

> My lofty thoughts reach up to the heavens;
> But on earth I am humiliated, frustrated, and agonized.
> I am unable to manage the affairs of this world,
> And I constantly face stumbling-blocks in this path.
> Why are the affairs of the world beyond my control?
> Why is the learned in religion a fool in the affairs of the world?

and he gets the following shattering answer:

> Anyone who [claims to be able to] walk on the heavens;
> Why should it be difficult for him to stalk on the earth?[6]

Positively, Iqbāl hardly gave anything that can be called a formulation of Muslim educational policies. Not only in education but also in other fields of human endeavor, Iqbāl left no positive legacy except that he wanted an autonomous homeland for the Muslims (what is now Pakistan), so that they might be able to organize and direct their lives according to the precepts of Islam. Perhaps it was not his task to formulate policies; his performance consisted in arousing the Muslim and stirring him to the core so that he could find for himself, amid the bewildering maze of modern theories, doctrines, and practices, a definite direction with specific policies to realize Islam on earth. What happened subsequently we shall study in the following chapter; here we must now turn to delineating the major practical developments that occurred in this field before the middle of the twentieth century.

6. Ibid., pp. 189, 190.

Practical Modernist Reforms

School Education

We saw in the previous section that it was easier for the Ottomans to set up professional academies of higher learning—medical, engineering, and such—than to reform primary and secondary education, particularly the former, which was kept under the control of the madrasa system right up until the beginning of the present century. In my general remarks in the preceding section, I also observed that a country like Turkey, which preserved itself from falling under foreign rule, direct or indirect, faced much greater difficulty, and took longer in modernization than did Egypt or the subcontinent of India when the latter came under direct British rule. This can be seen from the fact that Muḥammad ʿAlī of Egypt was able to establish a modern government school system earlier than the Ottomans. However, the Egyptian schools recruited pupils mostly from alien and non-Muslim nationalities (which, despite some foreign-modeled secular institutions in Turkey, would have been impossible in that country). When the Egyptian Muslims did go to Muḥammad ʿAlī's schools, they were more or less conscripted and, as a result, came mostly from the lower classes.

In Turkey, since the ulema were so resistant to change, bridges were created in the middle and the later years of the nineteenth century between the primary and higher education in the form of *rüshdiye,* or intermediate schools, which also, of course, had religious content in their curriculum. But while the problem in Turkey throughout the nineteenth century was how to introduce secular education at all, or how to weaken the hold of the clerics on education, the problem in Egypt in the latter half of that century (when Egyptian Muslims began to attend the general educational systems) was exactly the opposite, namely, how to make this school system (which had been both foreign-tailored and foreign-manned) more attuned to the religious, cultural, and national needs of Egypt. For Muḥammad ʿAlī's primary reason for establishing these schools had been to produce personnel for government and administration, not to produce a person imbued with Islamo-Egyptian culture; and those graduates who could not secure such employment (and they were the majority) were ill-equipped to earn a livelihood—a case strikingly similar to the products of the British system of education in

India. Thus, Muḥammad ʿAbduh wrote criticizing the government systems of school education:

> [This education is imparted so that the student] may have in his hand a degree which would make it possible for him to occupy a clerical chair in a department. But that his personality should be shaped by education and by the inculcation of values so that he becomes a good and proper man in himself, so that he should well execute the task entrusted to him in the government or outside it, this fact enters the minds neither of the teachers nor of those who appoint those teachers.[7]

And we are told the following about the primary government schools:

> The students of these schools until now continue to be those children whose guardians' aim in educating them is to attain government service, whether they realize their goal or not. . . . [In the latter case], the child returns to his father or his guardian after finishing his books, having learned the elements of sciences for which he cannot find any application. . . . He then degenerates into a moral state worse than those illiterate persons who nevertheless had remained in their natural condition; and, frustrated, he finds that he is unable to do the work that his father and family were engaged in. Thus he spends out his life either in total unemployment or nearly so.[8]

The poet Ḥālī, although he had been instrumental in the propagation of Sayyid Aḥmad Khān's policy of encouraging Indian Muslims to adopt modern British education, nevertheless in his poem *Musaddas* criticizes the product of that policy in much the same forms that Muḥammad ʿAbduh applied to the Egyptian educational system:

> They neither can make their mark in government service,
> Nor can they utter a word in the high Durbar
> Nor yet can they haul goods on their backs in the bazaar;
> And no longer are they able to till fields, either!
> Were they not "educated" they could have earned livelihood

7. Muḥammad ʿAbduh, *al-Aʿmāl al-Kāmila,* ed. Muḥammad ʿImāra, 6 vols. (Beirut: Al-muʾassasah al-ʾarabiyyah li-l-dirāsāt wa-l-nashr, 1972), 3:111.
8. Ibid.

in a hundred ways
But they are completely lost—thanks to their "education"![9]

In Turkey modern primary education, as I mentioned earlier, was not introduced until about 1908. By the 1913 primary education ordinance, primary education was divided into three classes: elementary, primary, and vocational-technical; but the implementation of the law suffered from lack of adequate teachers in the technical field. Nevertheless the law was a major step in departing from the traditional, purely religious primary education toward a practical concept of education. Religion, of course, continued to be taught until it was eliminated from the public school system under the republic. Between 1913 and 1919, girls' education was also organized on a practical basis, the major subject being home economics. Another major step toward the nationalization of primary education was taken by the 1913 law in its requirement that all education be in the Turkish language, whereas according to a law of 1879 each religious community (*millet*) could use its own language as the medium of instruction.

Indeed, the period from the early 1900s through the second constitutional period was a period of general intellectual and spiritual restlessness and awakening in Turkey, and all aspects of life—the family institution, economy, politics, and education—came under discussion. It was a period of free speech. In the field of primary education, certain nonmadrasa public orators for the first time gave their message to the masses in such an uninhibited fashion that Niyazi Berkes has characterized them as "effective eccentrics."[10] The central theme of their preaching was exhortation to move the body—stand erect, run, wrestle (all these were violent affronts to the traditional conception of calm dignity)—the open ridicule of certain settled habits, and the glorification of the arts. So strong was this movement that even madrasas are said to have adopted gymnastics. Riza Tevfik (1868–1949), Selim Sirri (1874–1957), and Ismail Hakki Baltacioğlu (1889–), whom I mentioned in the previous section in connection with the advocacy of a purely secular school education, typify this type of orator. The noted humanist deist Tevfik Fikret (1867–1915) announced, on assuming the directorship of

9. Khwāja Alṭaf Ḥusain Ḥālī, *Musaddas,* (Luknow: Ṣadi, 1935), p. 72.
10. Berkes, *Development of Secularism in Turkey,* p. 407.

the lycée of Galatasaray, his policy of religious educational reform by purging religion of superstitious beliefs, basing it instead on reason and science, and thereby healing the divorce between the world and religion created by the ulema.[11]

It should be noted that this was the call of most Muslim modernists as distinguished from the secularists, and it should be further borne in mind that Fikret's naturalism hardly differed from Sayyid Aḥmad Khān's in India. Yet the opposition of the Turkish Islamists to Fikret was far less than that of the Indian Muslim conservatives had been to the ideas of Sayyid Aḥmad Khān. Indeed, by that time many, if not all, of the Turkish ulema had come to accept the idea that the Turkish youth should get an education that would imbue his character with both nationalist and scientific spirit. It was against this background of the debate between the Islamist, the Westernist, the liberal individualist, and those who stood for technical education that, as I indicated in the previous section, Zia Gökalp appeared as the champion of a nationalist point of view that included the administration of Islamic values as expressed through Turkish mores to the Turkish youth—what he called *tarbiya* (upbringing or personality molding)—in addition to and as distinct from "education," which was supposed to be "objective" and "purely scientific."

However, by the law of 3 March 1924, called "the Law of Unification of Education," all religious schools and madrasas, run either by the Ministry of Awqāf (Pious Endowments) or even by private awqāf, were closed. Whereas the Tanzimat reformers had created a dualism between religious and secular instruction and proposals were subsequently made, particularly by the sadrazam (chief minister) Said Paša to reform the madrasas and to convert them into the theological faculties of his proposed universities, Atatürk's government, under the claim of "unifying" all education, eliminated the traditional schools, and thus all education became "this-worldly" or "secular." That is, "unification" was achieved not by integration or synthesis but by simply eliminating one of the two terms. The training of religious functionaries—imāms and khatībs—was continued under the aegis of the Ministry of Education, but this was eliminated in 1928 when all religious education was dropped from the public school system. Not until the late forties and early fifties was Islamic

11. Ibid.

education resumed, when, under sheer public pressure, a new system of imām-khatīb schools was started that, as we shall see in the next chapter, has expanded greatly up to the present.

Thus we see that Turkey and Egypt, as far as religious school education is concerned, moved in opposite directions during the first half of this century. In Egypt, under the criticism of Muḥammad ʿAbduh and others, a public school system that had been purely secular in its genesis under Muḥammad ʿAlī incorporated courses in Islam in order to become more Islamic and national. In Turkey, on the other hand, a purely traditional school system gave way, in the twenties, to a system that was absolutely secular by design—and with a vengeance. Since the developments in Egypt occurred naturally rather than by suppression, the integration of religious and secular education ran more smoothly; in Turkey religious education was expunged from the curriculum of the public schools for about a quarter of a century. Most modernized Turks whom we meet today outside Turkey, particularly in the West—although of course many of them have received some Islamic education either at home or in private schools—are products of this purely secular system, whose two chief architects, Kemāl Atatürk and Ismet Inönü, considered it a violation of the sanctity of the secularist principle even to mention the word "Allah" in public! Let us now turn to a brief consideration of higher Islamic education during the first half of the present century.

Higher Education

I indicated in chapter 1 that in the seventeenth and eighteenth centuries, particularly in the latter, secular learning—mathematics, chemistry, astronomy, medicine, philosophy, and so on—existed both in Turkey and in Egypt, and it appears that the increasing resistance of the ulema to change was most probably linked with the pressures felt by the Muslim world from the colonial or quasi-colonial experiences. The more the threat of the Western powers and their "advisers" resulted in the creation of centers of purely secular learning, the more the ulema assumed a defensive posture and took refuge in their inheritance from the later Middle Ages and its sterile commentatorial literature. Nevertheless, unlike the situation in Turkey, there arose in Egypt a series of men who took up the work of the reform of al-Azhar. Already during the first half of the nineteenth century, an Azhari shaykh, Rifāʿa al-Ṭahṭāwī, who had lived for a number of years in Paris, opened a college of languages and translated the French constitution and French civil law into Arabic. He also was probably the first to contend, in his work *Manāhij al-Albāb,* that Muslims must learn all the modern sciences, since Europeans had developed them after borrowing them from Muslims themselves. He was highly critical of Muḥammad ʿAlī for not including these sciences in the current Azhar curriculum, although in the past they had been taught there. But the painful process of reform can perhaps be best illustrated in the words of the greatest of Azhar reformers, Shaykh Muḥammad ʿAbduh:

> After attending Sayyid Jamāl al-Dīn al-Afghānī's lectures I turned my attention to the problem of the reform of al-Azhar since I was a student there. When I [actually] began work, I was prevented from it. . . . Then, after my return from exile, I tried to convince Shaykh Muḥammad al-Anbābī, then Shaykh al-Azhar, to accept cetain proposals, but he refused. Once I said to him, "Would you agree, O Shaykh, to order that the *Muqaddima* of Ibn Khaldūn be taught at al-Azhar? and I described to him whatever I could of the benefits of this work. He replied, "It would be against the tradition of teaching at al-Azhar." During our intricate conversation, I began talking to him about some more recent shaykhs, i.e., professors of al-Azhar, and asked him, "How long ago did al-Ashmūnī and al-Ṣabbān die?" He replied that they had died only so many years ago. I then said, "They have died only recently and yet their books are being taught and there had been no tradition of teaching them." Shaykh al-Anbābī was silent and did not reply.[12]

Al-Azhar went through a series of organizational and administrative reforms from 1872 to 1930, beginning with the requirement of a final examination resulting in a degree (called al-ʿĀlimiya), determining the hierarchy, salaries, and scales of its teachers, and finally creating three fields of instruction—theology, Islamic law, and Arabic language and literature (1930). But my purpose in this work is to study intellectual developments rather than administrative reforms. However, critiques such as those of Muḥammad ʿAbduh and of Muḥammad ibn Ibrāhīm

12. ʿAbduh, *al-Aʿmal al-Kāmila,* 3:177.

al-Ẓawāhirī in his *Kitāb al-ʿIlm wa-l-ʿUlamāʾ* (*The Book of Scholarship and Scholars*), issued from Ṭanṭā in 1905, show that even the law of 1872 was very imperfectly implemented. Of these two critiques, that of Muḥammad ʿAbduh (see his *al-Aʿmal al-Kāmila*, ed. Muḥammad ʿUmara, [Beirut, 1972], 3:112–14, 177–97) is obviously more radical: he thinks of reform in terms of a primarily intellectual and positive renaissance of Islam, while al-Ẓawāhirī's conception of the reform of al-Azhar is more in pietistic terms. Both agree, however, that the law governing the examination is poorly applied, that students loiter around without attending lectures, that most teachers are engaged in running each other down and showing themselves off rather than in teaching students, and that both students and teachers are content with minimal standards. Al-Ẓawāhirī rightly points out that the ulema are not just professionals like the holders of the degrees in engineering or other professions, for upon their shoulders lies the task of the moral leadership of society. Therefore for the holders of the ʿĀlimiya degree to pride themselves on it and to stop building upon it by further acquisition of knowledge and improvement of character detracted from their standing as ulema and degraded them in the eyes of the public.

During the last quarter of the nineteenth century and the early years of the twentieth, the intellectual-spiritual milieu at al-Azhar was, on the whole, very conservative. The khedival politics and intrigues (the palace was certainly not a friend of Muḥammad ʿAbduh's ideas) certainly played their part, but even without these the pace of progress was slow, since most shaykhs, even if they fully understood the meaning of the reforms, were averse to them, and many thought they would undermine Islam. ʿAbduh himself insisted on gradual reform only and was particularly anxious to keep al-Azhar independent of government interference. We can guess something of al-Azhar's milieu from a story told by al-Ẓawāhirī. A Lebanese Muslim, having heard of the great learning of al-Anbābī, who was rector of al-Azhar, journeyed to Egypt to see him (this must have been in the 1890s), and when the intermediary introduced the visitor to the shaykh as having traveled from Lebanon, the shaykh replied by asking, "Where is Lebanon?" or rather, "Where is Mount Lebanon?" since the story dates from the time when Lebanon was part of

Syria and was known as Mount Lebanon. The visitor then exclaimed, "By God! I have wasted every step I took to visit the shaykh!"[13]

ʿAbduh himself was disappointed in the reform of al-Azhar and, in view of the rigidity of the al-Azhar curriculum, began advising the government to set up a separate college for training lawyers (Dār al-Qaḍāʾ) independent of al-Azhar. When, finally, ʿAbduh was forced to resign from the Council of al-Azhar in March 1905, Shaykh al-Sharbīnī, the rector of al-Azhar, said, "The aim of our forefathers in setting up al-Azhar was to establish a 'house of God,' that is, a mosque wherein He would be worshiped. . . As for the worldly affairs and modern learning, they have nothing to do with al-Azhar. . . . That man [ʿAbduh] wanted to destroy the clear paths of religious instruction and to convert this great mosque into a school of philosophy and literature."[14] The khedive ʿAbbās II spoke in a similar vein on the occasion of Sharbīnī's installation as Shaykh al-Azhar. The distance between the two aforementioned critics of al-Azhar, ʿAbduh and al-Ẓawāhirī, can be seen from the fact that the latter's ideal as an ʿālim would be a person "who combines in himself the qualities of an ʿAbduh and a Sharbīnī!" There is little doubt or even wonder that, to many of his contemporary reformers and even "progressives," ʿAbduh must have seemed a pure secularist out to destroy Islam; yet it would still take some imagination to fuse ʿAbduh and Sharbīnī into a single personality!

It was, indeed, ʿAbduh who boldly expressed the view that al-Azhar might be merged into the general educational system—as the center of Islamic education—instead of remaining a curious enclave or museum of Islamic medievalism and, further, that after the institutions of learning in the general education system are duly reformed (see the preceding section of this chapter) and genuine and effective Islamic instruction is introduced in them, the importance of al-Azhar will, in any case, diminish because "people send their children to al-Azhar [instead of public schools] since they believe that al-Azhar better preserves their faith for them."[15] It needs to be pointed out with some emphasis that ʿAbduh contended not only for the introduction of modern

13. *Taʾrīkh al-Azhar wa-taṭawwurihī* (Cairo: Ministry of Awqāf, 1964), p. 20.
14. Ibid., p. 259.
15. ʿAbduh, *al-Aʿmāl al-Kāmila,* 3:114.

Western learning into al-Azhar, but—what is not generally recognized or understood—for the revival of old and original Islamic classics (witness his desire for the inclusion of Ibn Khaldūn's *Muqaddima* into the curriculum), including the theological works of the rationalist Muʿtazila school, which had been boycotted for centuries as heretical. Indeed, to rediscover "modernity" in the original Islamic tradition itself was a cornerstone of ʿAbduh's reformist thinking.

When the 1872 law of Al-Azhar was promulgated under the shaykhhood of Muḥammad al-ʿAbbāsī al-Mahdī, the following eleven areas were named as examination subjects: Islamic law (fiqh), Islamic jurisprudence, theology, Ḥadīth, Qurʾān exegesis (note the absence of the teaching of the Qurʾān by itself—untied to commentaries—a characteristic of all medieval institutions of Islamic learning), Arabic syntax and morphology, and the three sciences of rhetoric, eloquence and literary style, and logic. With regard to logic (philosophy was of course banned), although the controversy persisted concerning the advisability of teaching a subject that "was intermixed with philosophy," it continued to be taught as an "instrumental science" because of the aid it afforded to correct thinking processes. In 1887 a government-inspired question was put to the Shaykh al-Azhar, al-Anbābī, whether it was permissible, indeed necessary, for Muslims to acquire such sciences as mathematics, astronomy, physics, and chemistry "to increase the capacity of the Muslim community to compete with contemporary nations." In the question, an appeal was made to the authority of al-Ghazālī, who had written that it was obligatory upon the community *as a whole* to ensure that a sufficient number of its members study these sciences, and to the fact that scholars of the Ḥanafī school had agreed with al-Ghazālī's view. The questioner also took care to add that the position of these natural sciences would be that of "instrumental sciences" like logic, which are studied not for their own sake but for the benefits that accrue from them. (Compare the "useful knowledge" concept in Turkey discussed earlier in this chapter.) Al-Anbābī, who knew the real source of this question, affirmed in his answer that it was necessary for Muslims to study these sciences, warning, however, that "astronomy should not be studied for astrological purposes and that physics should be studied in conformity with the *Sharīʿa* and not in the way of the [medieval Muslim] philosophers, since that would be unlawful."[16] By "the way of the philosophers," of course, the shaykh meant such doctrines as the eternity of the world and, implicitly, the eternity of the laws of nature, which might undermine the belief in the hereafter.

Shaykh al-Anbābī had, of course, no intention of carrying out this reform, since, as we have seen, he was even opposed to the study of Ibn Khaldūn's *Muqaddima,* which ʿAbduh proposed later than this fatwā (ʿAbduh returned from exile in 1888). The implementation came in 1896, but the new sciences were made optional for the final examination. When in 1907, as ʿAbduh had proposed, a separate college was established for training experts in Islamic law to function in religious courts, the Azharis really saw the danger signal and realized the necessity of reform. The law of 1908 made obligatory the examination in the "modern" sciences—history, geography, mathematics, physics, and chemistry—as well as in the religious sciences. However, when the 1911 law raised the period of instruction from twelve to fifteen years and divided it into three levels (primary, secondary, and advanced), the teaching of these "modern" sciences was restricted to the first two levels, leaving the advanced level entirely for "religious" sciences. Philosophy, so much dreaded by the ulema, was not brought into the curriculum until 1930, and later both ancient and modern philosophy, including psychology and sociology, began to be taught. But again these new branches of knowledge were taught only in the lower levels, so that their instruction, except in rare and individual cases, remained very superficial. For a wholesale modernization of al-Azhar we have to await the 1960s and 1970s.

Despite its limitations, however, the progress of al-Azhar by the law of 1936 (which supplemented the 1930 measures) had come a long way from 1872. The development of the ability of religious thought to cope with the modern challenges is a problem that has baffled experts and will continue to do so, but it seems to me that for a life-oriented and socially geared religion like Islam it is more necessary to teach philosophy and social sciences than the individual physical sciences (except at the elementary level) at the highest possible level. But there are other practical demands to be met, and I shall discuss this particular

16. *Taʾrikh al-Azhar,* pp. 249–50.

question more fully in the next chapter. For the time being I shall turn to developments in the eastern lands of Islam, after a few remarks about Turkey.

In the preceding section I have discussed lower education in Turkey, culminating in the Kemālist closure not only of religious schools but of all religious teaching in the public school system. There is not much more to be said of the higher Islamic education except that, during the reign of Ạbdul Hamīd II, the prime minister (sadrazam) Said Paša drew up a grand proposal for setting up, in every provincial capital of the Ottoman empire, a university and an institution of higher technological learning (the one fed by the sültaniye schools and the other by the rüshdiye schools), with all higher institutions of religious learning (Islamic, Christian, etc.), becoming theological faculties in the universities for each respective religious community. This grand scheme did not materialize, and, after the abortive closing of the Dār al-Funūn mentioned earlier in this chapter, madrasas and secular educational institutions operated side by side. In 1909 (about fifteen years after the formal, though as yet nominal introduction of modern sciences into al-Azhar) the original madrasa of Muḥammad (Mehmet) the Conqueror was revived with the hope from both sides (the Westernists and the Islamists) of putting through a synthesized and reformed curriculum. This institution was to have four faculties—religious sciences (which, besides traditional subjects, included ethics), *ḥikmat*-sciences (comprising philosophy, mathematics, and all the natural sciences), the science of history (including the Prophet's biography), and languages (Arabic, Turkish, and Persian).

When the Shaykh al-Islām attempted, on this pretext, to extend his authority of censorship beyond his powers, this led in 1916 to the removal of religious education (among other things) from his control. Religious education was thus given over to the Ministry of Education. The most striking feature throughout the educational developments in Turkey has been the identification of the religious with the eternal and unchangeable and the secular with the changeable. This has been the real bane of Turkish Islam—a continuous expansion of the "secular" and a concomitant relegation of the "religious" to the background. It is this confusion that also haunted the thinking of Gökalp, who drafted the proposal for the 1916 law. Ottoman Turkey lacked a central madrasa like al-Azhar and, what is far more important, a modernist ʿālim like ʿAbduh. The law of 1916 was destined to be the first step toward that "unification of education" that Muṣṭafā Kemāl completed by abolishing religious education: the unchangeable vanished before the changeable! It remained for Muṣṭafā Ṣabrī, the last Shaykh al-Islām, who emigrated to Egypt, to write a multivolume work in defense of Ashʿarī predestinarianism, while much earlier ʿAbduh had resurrected, despite fierce opposition, human free will and a rationalistic approach to religion in Egypt.

Two important general points deserve notice concerning modern developments, the first related to all "historical" lands of Islam, that is, the Middle East, North Africa, Turkey, Iran, and the subcontinent, or, rather more precisely, in terms of Arabic, Turkish, Persian, and Urdu languages. In all these languages, the medieval style was artificial, ornate, and difficult to understand, and the content was unoriginal, characterized by obscurity of expression rather than expression of obscurity. Apart from artificial trends in pure literature, in both poetry and prose, the so-called language sciences mentioned in the first chapter—eloquence, rhetoric, and "style," with the artificial and farfetched devices, images, similes, and constructions produced by them—put a heavy and often distasteful emphasis on expression at the expense of meaning. The commentatorial character of the later writings in the field of nonliterary or technical learning compounded the viciousness of these trends and added to them an often-obnoxious pedantic air. One common feature of the new literary reform that affected all teaching during the nineteenth and twentieth centuries was the simplification of style into a direct and natural one. In the field of Islamic literature and education in particular the names of Cevdet Paša and Namik Kemāl in Turkey, ʿAbduh and his colleagues in Egypt, Sayyid Aḥmad Khān, Ḥālī and others in the subcontinent stand out. The emergence of the popular press, of course, both reflected and affected this development. The new reformed style had a great impact on all branches of learning, particularly in ethics, history, geography, and such. This in itself is a major, indeed, basic, revolution. In all these languages, poetry—the real magic of the oriental mind—was effectively used for reform purposes, and the new, easily accessible style helped the whole cause of reform and education. In the subcontinent, it was Alṭāf Ḥusayn Ḥālī (a right-hand man of Aḥmad Khān) who set the pioneering example followed by Muḥammad Iqbāl. The influence of Ḥālī's (d. 1914) *Musaddas*—a moving poem on the fall of Islam consisting of stanzas of six lines each, with its realism and stark sincerity, its direct and pungent style—has been incalculable in Indian Islam in terms of arousing Muslims to their plight of insufferable decline and decay. While this poem is essentially a critique of literally all segments and strata of Indian Muslim society, it was Iqbāl's "grand style" poetry that moved people to action.

The second general point to be remembered is that the thousand-year-old ulema tradition, despite its stagnation in the later centuries, had nevertheless a rich and highly sophisticated heritage. It could boast of a thousand original personalities, highly synthetic and creative figures in the various fields of the vast Islamic civilization. Even the commentators, while they more or less effectively lost their grasp on the bases of the sciences, nevertheless were often expert in their fields—up to their minutiae. Now, whenever a major change occurs in an educational system by the introduction of new subjects, the standards are bound to go down simply because it takes time to attain expertise in the new fields. If the new subjects are organically related to the old ones, the backlash is not so big and the hiatus not so long, since the whole develops and rises as a whole. In the Muslim world, however, the new education did not start out integrated with the old, since the representatives of old education did not want this, nor, in most cases, did the espousers of the new. For this reason the two remained mostly segregated for a long time, and in many countries they still remain so.

A further complicating factor was that this new education had been transplanted from another living organism in Europe, with its own cultural background and its own internal structure and consistency. Although this had happened earlier to Islam with the influx of Greek philosophy and science into the Islamic intellectual and spiritual stream, the main difference from the present situation was that the Greek civilization was dead while the Islamic civilization was alive and powerful and hence could face the challenge of the Greek sciences on its own terms. But Islamic civilization confronted modern Western sciences at a multiple disadvantage—psychological as well as intellectual—because of the political domination, economic aggression, and intellectual hegemony of the West. I have pointed out earlier—

and this is important to remember—that the present Islamic conservatism is to be explained in no small measure by the colonial interregnum and the primarily psychological complications it created for the upholders of traditional education.

Both the old and the new types of education suffered from the absence of mutual integration, but the new was damaged most, at least in the short run. Because of its foreign provenance and lack of rootedness in the new culture, the new education suffered for several generations. Because of the poor quality of the early graduates of the new education relative to the old—which had several centuries of proud if not always productive history—the former were scoffed at for a long time, both for being creatures of foreign influence and for their lack of originality *in their own field of education.*

Nowhere perhaps were these features more prominent than in the Muslim subcontinent. The characterization of the products of the new education as bloodless, pale shadows of the West and as cultural-intellectual bastards was a patent theme with Abūʾl-Kalām Āzād and the poet Akbar Allāhābādī, though there were many others who indulged in it. Sayyid Aḥmad Khān himself described the early products of Aligarh as "Satans." As for their lack of originality and usefulness to their societies, this idea was strongly expressed by Ḥālī, Shiblī Nuʿmānī, and Iqbāl. The derogatory term *maghrib zadah* (West-stricken) was applied to the modern-educated and Westernized classes by many writers, the most prominent of them being Āzād, Ẓafar ʿAlī Khān, and Mawdūdī. We must also remember that the largest sector of the new education was that of liberal arts, and its object was to create officials and servants for the *British government in India.* Science was studied by very few, owing to lack of industry, wherein the colonial regime undoubtedly played the most basic role, and hence the institutions overflowed with liberal arts graduates. People could be seen in, say, Lahore with the M.A. degrees, shining shoes on the steps of a petty shop. It was this poor quality of the new graduate and his utter uselessness and helplessness that was highlighted, for example, by Ḥālī in his *Masuddas* in lines quoted earlier.

We shall see in the next chapter that this situation has improved and that Muslims educated in the modern disciplines are coming closer to the standards of their Western models; indeed, educational modernity in this sense is no longer identified with the

West but must be termed simply "modernity." But it is of capital importance to remember in the same breath exactly what area it is in which the Muslim world is fast closing its gap with the West. It is either in pure physical sciences or in technological skills. Even there the gap, of course, remains large, but it is essentially a matter of time and financial resources, and given these it will certainly be closed. The social sciences (*sciences humaines*) are in their infancy in the Muslim world, although they are rather young even in the West. The more these sciences become divorced from an intellectual philosophical base in the West, the more easily and quickly will the Muslims fill up the gap between themselves and the West. Further, as I shall elaborate more fully in the next chapter, Muslims have begun to realize that social sciences as developed in the West are tied to certain perspectives and mostly unexpressed values that Muslims may not be able to espouse. It is a question, for example, whether a Muslim psychiatrist or psychologist can with equanimity go along with many of his Western counterparts who, to relieve pressure on the psyche of their subjects, would readily denude them of all morality because they see this morality as having been extrinsically drummed up in the first place.

However, it is in the field of pure thought or philosophical intellectualism that the Muslim remains underdeveloped. It is not an accident that in the entire gamut of Islamic modernism the only serious student of philosophy the Muslim world can boast of is Muḥammad Iqbāl. But it is also true that this intellectualism has experienced a palpable decline in the West itself, particularly since World War II. The story of how pure technology has almost stifled liberal humanism, with the social sciences precariously sandwiched between the two, is too recent to tell, and its effects on Western civilization have just begun to appear. It is this Western educational culture—a house swept almost bare—then, with which the Muslim world is trying more or less successfully to catch up. The ulema's traditional intellectual culture has declined greatly since the advent of modern education, but the Western intellectual culture has also declined and is in crisis. Let us now follow up briefly and specifically the story of the traditional Islamic intellectual culture vis-à-vis modern education in the subcontinent.

It was Warren Hastings, the British ruler of Eastern India, who in 1781 founded the Madrasa ʿĀliya (the higher madrasa) in Calcutta that has survived to this day. Under what seems to have been deliberate policy, classical Muslim sciences—astronomy, mathematics, philosophy—were introduced into it. Since, however, these were not modern Western, but medieval Muslim sciences and since the perspective thus was historical rather than systematic, the institution, although it gave serious instruction, had little impact on religious thought. After 1947 a madrasa of the same name was established in Bangladesh (former East Pakistan); in the 1930s a number of "reformed madrasas" were set up in Bengal with a certain mixture—somewhat varying in proportion—of traditional Islamic and modern subjects, but on the whole these were not regarded as very successful and were judged to fall between two stools.

By far the most important educational institution in India was, of course, the Aligarh College that was established by Sayyid Aḥmad Khān in 1881 and became a university in 1920. But, as I said in the previous section on theoretical modernism, although modern disciplines were taught at Aligarh—especially in the early stages—by British and other European professors, the teaching of Islam had to be given over to a traditionalist scholar from Deoband owing to the large-scale opposition to Sayyid Aḥmad Khān's personal religious views and to those of his nuclear group. As a result, the modern never really met with the traditional, which remained extremely peripheral to the academic life of the institution. As is very well known, however, it was Aligarh that produced the bulk of Muslim graduates in modern learning right up until 1947 and that also served as the nerve center of the Muslim nationalist movement leading to the creation of Pakistan. Since independence, the Indian government has taken a series of measures to "reform" Aligarh, basically bringing in large numbers of non-Muslim, especially Hindu, students. Concerning the dream of Sayyid Aḥmad Khān, however, to refertilize Islamic thought and create a new science of theology vibrant with a new and potent Islamic message, Aligarh was doomed to failure from the very start.

Some important further experiments were made, some taking modern education as their starting point and therefore being essentially modern and attempting to accommodate as much as possible of traditional Islamic learning, while others took the opposite course. Again, the combination in each case was somewhat different, and each major institution developed a different emphasis. In 1917 the Osmania University was founded in Hyderabad, Deccan, named after the niẓām of the Deccan, Osman ʿAlī Khān. Although it included several courses on Islam and though examinations were held in Islamic law, jurisprudence, Ḥadīth, Qur'ān commentary, and theology, the treatment of these subjects was superficial and even peripheral to the mainstream of modern education. The remarkable and distinguishing feature of this university was that all instruction, including higher teaching and professional training (law and medicine) was in Urdu. Consequently all textbooks were translated into Urdu. However, owing to the limited number of works in Urdu on modern subjects and to the lower standard of English—in which there was a wealth of material in all fields—Osmania was unable to compete with the other Indian universities, whose medium of instruction was English. As a result, many Muslim students from Hyderabad itself came to Aligarh. If most Muslim educational institutions had followed the example of the Osmania, after a temporary fall in standards the level should have risen again, and long before today Muslim identity in the subcontinent also could have been strengthened immeasurably.

But owing partly to the British presence in India and partly to the fear that Muslims might be disadvantaged against Hindus if they let their standards fall even temporarily, Muslims, along with Hindus, went in the wrong direction at this critical stage of their educational development. Indeed, the subcontinent is a land without a language. As a result Muslims have suffered an incalculable cultural loss. Those Indo-Pakistani Muslims who criticize the Turks for cutting themselves off from their past by adopting a new script should rather search their own hearts and see if they have not cut themselves off far more effectively from the whole of their own religious-intellectual higher cultural roots by practically refusing to develop Urdu into an adequate medium of higher instruction and of scientific and philosophic thought. If there are today practically, and indeed dangerously, two nations in Pakistan, it is not only because the religious leadership has little contact with the demands of a modern society, but even more so because of the cultural bastardy of the Westernized classes. There is absolutely no question that the teeming millions of Muslims will never learn English and that the culturally Western-oriented classes will ever remain a tiny minority.

How can a country survive, let alone prosper, with such cultural schizophrenia?

More successful than Osmania University were the publishing enterprises of the niẓām Osman ʿAlī Khān. The Dāʾirat al-Maʿārif, set up by the niẓām, has served Islamic scholarship immensely both by publishing a vast number of Islamic classics in almost all fields, particularly historical and religious texts, and by issuing the quarterly *Islamic Culture,* which is still in existence. There are now in addition three notable new Islamic quarterlies in the subcontinent, *Islamic Studies* from Islamabad, *Studies in Islam* from New Delhi, and *Hamdard Islamicus* from Karachi.

Sayyid Aḥmad Khān's educational energies too were not confined to the founding of the Aligarh College. He instituted, with his comrades, the Muslim Educational Conference, which held its annual sessions in different parts of the subcontinent and proved an effective inspiration to take education seriously. Colleges and schools sprouted all over the country with curricula that were basically modern but contained an important, yet largely ineffective, ingredient of Islamic instruction. The expression "ineffective," however, needs to be explained. While it could not, in the nature of the case, provide any extensive or intensive understanding of Islam to students, it at least gave them enough intellectual and spiritual food to keep their cultural and religious identity.

Before we go on to other new institutions and their salient characteristics, a word is in order on the subject of female education. Muslims have, throughout history, attended to the question of women's instruction within the terms defined by their culture. Thus, women's education took place mostly either in their own homes or in a home selected in a quarter. Subjects were exclusively religion and home economics, but many women have excelled in Islamic history from time to time in different fields—particularly poetry, Ḥadīth, and Sufism. In the late nineteenth century Ashraf ʿAlī Thānavī (d. 1942), a scholar from Deoband seminary, wrote an encyclopedic work for women called *Bihishtī Zewar* (*Jewelry of Paradise*), which gave exhaustive instruction on traditional lines, not only on Islamic subjects but on cookery and hygiene. This voluminous work, to which the author continued to make additions and which has passed through scores of editions, was customarily given by parents as part of her dowry to every bride who could read, and in the traditionalist circles the practice still continues.

Neither Muḥammad ʿAbduh nor Sayyid Aḥmad Khān, nor yet the classical Turkish Muslim modernists (like Cevdet Paša and Namik Kemāl) seem to have been in favor of giving a *modern* education to women, although they were all in favor of women's education on traditional and domestic lines. In his reply to the welcome address given him by the "[Muslim] women of the Punjab" (I have not been able to ascertain the date, but it was probably in the 1890s), Sayyid Aḥmad Khān strongly supported the traditional and practical education of women; he vividly described the manner and matter of this education in the three generations of "my mother, my own generation, and that of my daughters," and he highly praised it.[17] He said, however, "Their [women's] education did not contain those sciences that some people now want to introduce in imitation of Europeans. The learning that will be beneficial today to women is the same that benefited them in the past, namely, religion and practical morality. . . . I know only one woman who read with her father the [Persian] autobiography of the emperor Jahāngīr. But her friends taunted her saying "Lady! What will this benefit you? You should study instead the Book of God [the Qurʾān] and those of His Prophet [the Ḥadīth]." It was this [religious] sort of education that infused into the minds of girls goodness and piety, mercy, love, and good character, and it was just this education that sufficed them in matters both religious and worldly."[18]

However, it was not long before girls' education in the subcontinent developed along the lines of Turkey and Egypt. Three types of education may be distinguished, apart form the traditional education in homes. Several girls' schools were set up with a normal public school curriculum but with added Islamic subjects, like the boys' schools mentioned earlier. An example is the "girls' school-college" (Madrasat al-Banāt) in Lahore that is both a school and a college. Second, there have more recently sprung up separate sections for women within certain traditionalist madrasas; some of them give higher traditionalist instruction, but many stop at primary Islamic education and are no more

17. Nadhr Aḥmad, *Jāʾizah-yi Madāris-i ʾArabiyyah Islāmiyyah Maghribī Pākistān A survey of Arabic madrasas in West Pakistan,* (Lahore: Muslim Academy, 1972), pp. 649–50.

18. Ibid., p. 650.

than Qurʾān schools for girls. In the third place, there are standard public schools for girls that, like all public schools in Pakistan at present, have compulsory religious instruction up to grade eight.

Shiblī Nuʿmānī, who had cooperated closely with Sayyid Aḥmad Khān in the establishment of Aligarh, eventually broke with his elder comrade over educational policy and in 1894 helped establish the Nadwat al-ʿUlamāʾ (Assembly of Islamic Scholars) in Lucknow. The aim of this institution, whose graduates have made an impact on the religious field perhaps second only to the purely traditionalist seminary of Deoband, was definitely to train ulema with a certain modernist orientation, not to produce graduates of modern secular learning. It can be regarded as a *via media* between Deoband and Firangī Maḥal on the one hand and Aligarh on the other. It has a sixteen-year program divided into grades ranging from primary education up to what it calls "specialization," which would be equivalent to a master of arts in secular universities. At the higher levels it teaches certain modern subjects, including some comparative religion and, to a limited extent, English langauge. It is doubtful if the teaching of modern subjects or English goes very far, but, owing to the institution's great emphasis on Arabic, its students seem to have easier access to both the classical Islamic works (the Arabic of other institutions, both new and old, is rather poor) and modern Islamic writings in the Arab world. This has brought it into influential contact with the Middle East, and its current head, Abuʾl-Ḥasan ʿAlī al-Nadvī, a devout preacher of Islam, not only has written in Arabic but has developed influence both on the Arab Middle East and, to some extent, on Turkey. The emphasis on Arabic is no doubt due to the influence of Shiblī Nuʿmānī, who was an eminent theologican, historian, and historian of literature as well as a litterateur and poet.

One beneficial effect of the refreshing emphasis on Arabic has been to bring into focus the original sources of Islam, the Qurʾān and the Ḥadīth—particularly the former. This was bequeathed by Shiblī's reformist activity to another madrasa founded in 1910 at Sarāi Mīr and called Madrasat al-Iṣlāh (Reformed Madrasa). Ḥamīd al-Dīn al-Farāhī, a well-known recent Qurʾān commentator, was its first head. This school also aimed at bringing together different schools of Sunni ulema, an earlier and somewhat nebulous form of what was later started more effectively at al-

Azhar under the name *al-Taqrīb bayn al-Madhāhib* (rapprochement among Islamic schools of law, including the Shīʿī school).

Neither of these two institutions, however, significant though they are, can be called modern Islamic institutions, since their modern element is either sorely lacking or dismally poor. A final institution originating before the partitioning of India in 1947 must be mentioned. In 1920 the Jāmiʿa Milliya Islāmiya (the National Islamic University) was founded near Delhi to satisfy three needs: Islamic instruction, modern education (with practical training in certain fields), and a strong Indian nationalist orientation. Aligarh was modern but not only was not nationalist but by policy was pro-British and was not in any real sense Islamic. Deoband was purely traditionalist Islamic and, since its founders had actively participated in the uprising of 1857, was by its background anti-British and nationalist. After Sayyid Aḥmad Khān's death, the pro-British policy of Aligarh also changed; particularly at the time of the founding of the Jāmiʿa Milliya Islāmiya, a Hindu-Muslim cooperation obtained against the British—the only time, in fact, that Hindus and Muslims cooperated. Its foundation stone was laid by the rector of Deoband, Maḥmūd al-Ḥasan, titled "shaykh al-Hind." The Islamic character of the Jāmiʿa was never very strong, since it never intended to produce ulema, and it gradually became still weaker, while during the thirties and forties its Indian nationalist orientation intensified. It still retains that character, although its Islamic character is more or less nominal.

In Iran, perhaps more than anywhere else, the tension between the religious establishment and the state has existed palpably from time to time since the latter half of the nineteenth century, most recently erupting fiercely in the Khomeini Revolution of 1979. The explanation for this does not seem to me to be that in Shīʿī Islam the state has little or no legitimacy in the absence of the imām—a thesis that has lately gained wide currency among Western scholars. These periodic conflicts and their severity do not seem to be a prominent feature of the Iranian situation during the Safavid period, but they became prominent in the late nineteenth century. Then the major cause and occasion seems to have been the sharp reaction of the ulema to the foreign encroachments on Iranian sovereignty, culminating in the Tobacco Concession protest and the constitutional struggle. It is interesting, however, that while the Egyptian ulema did not turn against the khedive when his policies came under British control in the 1880s but reacted against the British and while the ulema of India did not turn against the nominal Mogul ruler in Delhi but rebelled against the British usurpation of Muslim power, several leading Iranian ulema turned against their ruler over the tobacco issue, just as the Iranian religious leadership brought down Reza Shāh in 1979. The reason seems to be that the Iranian ulema saw their ruler as collaborating with a foreign power at the expense of their country, while in Egypt and India the rulers were preceived as having been overpowered by the foreign powers rather than as collaborating.

Observers have noticed that the Shīʿī ulema, on the whole, have played a more directly active and important role in political affairs and affairs of state than have their Sunni counterparts. The answer, again, seems to lie not in the so-called illegitimacy of the state in the eyes of the Shīʿī ulema but in the fact that the Shīʿī divines, ulema, and mujtahids appear to have a greater and much more direct influence on the masses than do Sunni ulema. This is perhaps to be explained by the fact that the Shīʿī religious representatives, by strongly appealing through effective rhetoric to the emotions of the public on the martyrdom of Ḥusayn (the Prophet's grandson)—which has become central to Shīʿī religion both at the lower level of passion plays and at the higher level of a refined ideal of suffering for the removal of injustice—are able to mobilize the Shīʿī public more easily and potently for what are perceived to be just and religious concerns.

It is this that also explains the lack of modernization of the subject matter of the traditional religious education in Iran and the ulema's resistance to it. In a way, of course, that traditional education had probably not suffered the same disintegration and decline in the later medieval centuries as had been experienced in the rest of the Muslim world. *Ḥikmat,* or philosophy, and other scientific subjects like mathematics and astronomy had continued to be taught and were not excised from the curriculum as they were elsewhere, particularly at al-Azhar. The philosophic tradition in particular has continued to be vigorous until the present day, and a Shīʿī mujtahid could therefore become a much more "rounded" or integrated and self-contained figure, educated in both traditional and rational disciplines.

During the reign of Reza Khān (Reza Shāh's father), a number of measures were promulgated in Iran, as elsewhere, to streamline education—for example, the grading of courses, the fixing of academic years, and an examination system. But while these reforms were accepted by the ulema, they resisted the dress law of 1930. The Shīʿī religious establishment has therefore been able to preserve its traditional character more or less intact and to withstand the pressure of the government to change it. It was a Shīʿī preacher who could publicly scold the queen (Reza Khān's wife) from the pulpit for letting her veil slip from her face during a religious function—although next day the shrine was raided by state police and the preacher humiliated.

But one important result of this persistence of virtually medieval education in Iranian madrasas has, of course, been that the knowledge of modern learning among the Shīʿī ulema is almost nonexistent. For this reason the quality of the ulema as well as their prestige and power has suffered increasingly in the face of progressive secularization of education. Nor were there in Iran new schools or madrasas like those of the Indian subcontinent that experimented with new curricula and syllabi in an attempt to synthesize the new and the old, each with its own character. The religious establishment at Qum continues to be the center and pride of religious education in Iran, but it is difficult to predict how long it will survive. I will further discuss the more recent developments in Iran in the next chapter.

The main developments of modern Islamic education in Indonesia fall in the period beginning about 1945—on the eve of independence—and will be dealt with in the next chapter, as will the case of Pakistan and the recent spectacular developments in Turkey. Here, therefore, I will make only brief remarks about Indonesia during the first half of this century. Up to about 1900, Islamic education in Indonesia was disseminated through local Qurʾān schools and *pesantrins*, the latter being of a lower caliber than the later madrasas and colleges, highly traditionalist in character and educating *santris*, that is, men versed in such religious knowledge as would render them competent to give fatwās (authoritative opinions on religious issues) and become functionaries in the mosques. The pesantrins were probably no better or worse than smaller madrasas in the subcontinent today, but they were more stable and self-contained organizationally in that they were usually set up outside villages, with agricultural land attached to them where students and teachers (who were boarders there) all worked corporately to support the institution.

By about 1900 intellectual influences from the Middle East began penetrating Indonesia. Indonesian pilgrims who had settled in Mecca or Medina and other teachers taught further incoming pilgrims from Indonesia who, after studying for a few years in the holy cities, went back to their country, setting up new pesantrins and higher-level madrasas. A little later, influence from Cairo became more powerful, and the impact of the reformist ideas of ʿAbduh and his school began to be felt. As a result, a conflict between the "conservatives" (*kaum tua*) and the "modernists" (*kaum muda*)—like the one that had occurred in Egypt itself—started in West Sumatra and subsequently spread to Java. The modernization entailed both the outward paraphernalia (like chairs, desks, and blackboards instead of mats on the ground) and the addition of new subjects to the traditional curriculum. The latter aspects, as expected already from the struggle in Egypt, were slow to be realized and did not gain much momentum until after 1930, when the pace of the introduction of modern knowledge, under the current Indonesian euphemism "general knowledge" (cf. the term "useful knowledge" used by early Ottoman reformers and the term "instrumental knowledge" used in Egypt), was accelerated.

The struggle between the conservatives and the modernists was institutionalized, as it were, by the formation in 1912 of the Muḥammadiya reformist group and by the setting up in 1926 of the Nahḍat al-ʿUlamāʾ; while the former was urban and represented progressive ideas of *ijtihād* (effort at personal thought) to cope with the changing situation, the latter was mainly based in the countryside and clung fast to the doctrines of the four classical schools (*madhāhib*) of Islamic law. It should be noted that the Muḥammadiya and their fellow travelers, influenced as they were by Egyptian modernism, were far ahead of the Deoband seminary or even the Nadwat al-ʿUlamāʾ in the subcontinent; surely some of their leaders and other like-minded personalities like Muḥammad Nāṣir (Natsir) have been much more progressive than the Jamāʿat-i-Islāmī of Pakistan. Indeed, a fundamental and interesting point of contrast between the Muḥammadiya and its cognates on the one hand and the Jamāʿat-i-Islāmī on the other is that while the latter, during its career in Pakistan (as distinguished from India), retrogressed, the former have shown a capacity for progressive development in their ideology. While this is highly important, it cannot be easily explained. The cause is probably at least partly (apart from the influence from Cairo) that, while the Muḥammadiya has had to compete with extra-Islamic groups and parties and has had to struggle—so far unsuccessfully—for the mere acceptance of the nomenclature "Islamic state," in Pakistan this nomenclature was available to start with. In the struggle to interpret what "Islamic state" means, the Jamāʿat, faced with the modernists' interpretation, gravitated progressively to a conservative position that eventually became indistinguishable from that of the traditionalist ulema. Indeed, the Indonesian madrasas and ulema have continuous links with al-Azhar, and also at present there are a large number of Indonesian students attending that institution. In the meantime, even the Nahḍat al-ʿUlamāʾ gives an excellent training in Arabic, at least in some of the major schools, thereby enabling students to pursue further studies in Egypt.

3

Contemporary Modernism

Introduction

I am starting this chapter from about the middle of the twentieth century, primarily because the independence of Muslim countries from the political hegemony of the West occurred about that time. The Muslim lands of Central Asia continue to be under the triple domination of communist Russia: political, economic, and—far more pernicious than any other form of colonialism known to history—intellectual-moral. But the Muslim struggle is alive there, and lately the new Russian czars seem to have realized that it is necessary to at least appear to relax the hitherto tight and forced isolation of the Central Asian Muslims from the rest of the Muslim world. In May 1977 an international conference of Muslims was held in Tashkent, where the Islamic potential for peace and the contribution of the "moral labor" of Muslims to world peace was discussed and celebrated. There is evidence that underground Islamic educational activities and religious propaganda of Muslims continue and eloquently proclaim that this genie will not be contained in the Marxist-Leninist bottle. However, little is known of the content of these educational activities that may one day be revealed.

Second, the political liberation of Muslim lands has meant that Muslims attempt to rethink the problem of education in their overall efforts to reconstruct their societies. This holds true for the bulk of the Muslim world that achieved political independence; some parts reached that point after a much grimmer struggle than others—often an armed struggle. But, as I indicated toward the end of the last chapter, Islamic education in Turkey also awoke at midcentury after a quarter-century's stupefying impact of Kemālist reformism. Even in Egypt, a truly and meaningfully new era dawned after the 1952 revolution and particularly after the 1956 "Suez affair." Such transforming experiences in the life of peoples have a vital impact on all important facets of life, even though on the surface they seem isolated.

Third, for these reasons, educational problems, including the problem of religious education, take on a realistic form and assume an immediacy that did not exist in the colonial interregnum, where both the privileges of and responsibilities for running the affairs of these societies rested basically with foreign powers. It is for these considerations that this chapter has been separated from the previous one and titled "Contemporary Modernism" in contrast to "Classical Modernism." For although that modernism was indeed concerned with internal reform—witness ʿAbduh and Aḥmad Khān, for example—it was equally involved in a controversialist reform with the West, while the postcolonial modernism of the contemporary period, in principle at least, is concerned basically and directly with internal reform and reconstruction. Also, because of this difference in the two situations, classical modernism could afford to be partial and unsystematic and could even afford to be slow—for at the theoretical level it was mostly a "defense of Islam" and hence chose to respond to those problems that the Western critics had raised, while at the practical level the urgency for a speedy and systematic reform was often difficult to feel owing to the absence of ultimate and concrete responsibilities for problem solving.

And yet, strange though it may seem, it is precisely this systematic working-out of Islam for the modern context that has not been forthcoming. In classical Islam, it had taken Muslims about two and a half to three centuries to accomplish a theological system, a legal-moral system, and a political system and then to administer them through a titanically controlled educational system to mold the orientation and ethos of the Muslim community. Indeed, this systematic structure and its educational ministration were so powerful and effective that, as an established tradition, they successfully obscured even the Qurʾān and the real performance of the Prophet from the learned Muslims (the ulema) themselves, let alone the "laymen" and massses. Admittedly, a period comparable to those three centuries or so is still very far away since the assumption of political self-determination by the Muslim world. But it is equally true that that kind of time span is surely neither available nor needed for a new systematic interpretation. It is also true that knowledge in the West itself has become so fragmented that it can hardly be called by that name, while during its early career Islam had available finished knowledge-products like Greek science and thought. Yet the crucial question to which we must eventually seek an answer here is whether there is an awareness among Muslims—and if so how much and how adequate—that an Islamic world view does need to be worked out today and that this is an immediate imperative; for unless such a system is attempted, there is little that can be ministered through education. But here precisely we come up against the most vicious of all circles of contemporary Islam—that unless necessary and far-reaching adjustments are made in the present system of education, it is not even conceivable that creative minds will arise that will work out the desired systematic interpretation of Islam. My main purpose, therefore, in this chapter is to outline the more recent developments in Islamic education so that, measuring by the yardstick of its performance in the Islamic past, we can come to some conclusions on where it is going. That is to say, we must answer the question of how far the current education is Islamically creative or indifferent or even negative vis-à-vis its putative goal.

Even its conceived goals at present are hardly fully or adequately stated anywhere. Muslim thinkers like Iqbāl have severely criticized Western education, as we saw in the previous chapter, as dehumanizing and numbing to the human spirit. But the current strategy, as we shall see presently, is not so much aimed at a positive goal; it seems rather to be a very defensive one: to save the minds of Muslims from being spoiled or even destroyed under the impact of Western ideas coming through various disciplines, particularly ideas that threaten to undermine the traditional standards of Islamic morality. Under these conditions of spiritual panic, the strategy universally evolved in the Muslim world is mechanical: in what proportion to combine certain "new" subjects with certain "old" ones so that the potion resulting from this chemistry will be "healthful"—that is, conducive to the technological benefits of modern civilization while avoiding the poison that threatens the moral fiber of Western society. I shall deal with this basic problem and this approach more fully in the next chapter; for the time being we shall study the educational systems being evolved in the contemporary Muslim world. As in the preceding chapter, I shall briefly analyze various salient Muslim countries in a way that might give us an overall picture and yield certain trends, despite the major differences of each country owing to historical and sociocultural factors.

The New Situation

By the "new situation" that begins about the middle of the twentieth century I mean certain basic politicoeconomic factors that were not present during the colonial or quasi-colonial period. Politically speaking, the major exception is Turkey, which had already ensured her political independence with the defeat of the Allies after World War I. All other major Muslim countries, including Egypt, became totally and practically sovereign in the political sense between 1947 and 1963. This brought the real political responsibility of the governing elite to the peoples of these new states. While this spelled a fundamental change in the political status of these countries, it meant even more important changes in terms of economic phenomena: all these countries began formulating and implementing schemes of economic expansion under the impact of the new ideology of economic development. For the first time economic (and other) development was "planned" by five- or four-year periods, and planning bodies in all "developing" countries started their task on a "scientific" footing with the new idea that development could be planned, oriented, and controlled. This was the meaning of "having control over one's own destiny"—the real fulfillment of political independence.

It appears that in those new countries where independence was won with mass involvement and with large-scale violence or armed conflict against the colonial power concerned, "socialist" tendencies appeared—that is, politicoeconomic trends that aimed at a greater participation of the poor masses in production and distribution. These socializing trends strengthened and were also strengthened by varying degrees of nationalism. In countries where this mass participation in armed conflict did not take place, socializing trends occurred after a few decades, in response to a pattern of economic development that tended to concentrate great economic wealth and power in the hands of a relatively small number of capitalists. Although one cannot deny that a goodly measure of prosperity and material well-being did percolate to the middle classes, the vastly increased economic gap between the upper and lower strata of these societies threatened to destroy them, a threat that resulted in an impetus to "socialization" or social-justice ideologies.

The ideology of planned economic development, of course, by itself implies that such development shall have a deliberately controlled orientation and not involve a totally laissez-faire society. But the socialistically oriented countries often resorted to wholesale and swift nationalization, not only of "basic industries" but of almost all channels of production, while those with a "liberal" economy aimed first of all at "creation of wealth" that could subsequently be subjected to distributive justice. But in situations where masses were ignorant and illiterate and a relatively small modern-educated elite claimed to be working on their behalf for their material prosperity, political freedoms were often curtailed both in "socialistic" and in "liberal" countries, since the rulers felt that political games would thwart quick economic development and in some cases threaten "the security of the state." Yet, as Gunnar Myrdal has correctly assessed in his *Asian Drama,* the governments of all these countries, whether dictatorships or democracies (and, of course, whether socialistic or liberal economies) are really unable to push development far enough and quick enough because they are inherently, in Myrdal's terms, "soft states," in the sense that they are unable to motivate and vitally mobilize their people for sufficient, speedy economic progress.

This brings us to the heart of our problem. The salient features of the new situation from our present perspective are: (1) that the governments of these countries, whether democracies or dictatorships, socialist-oriented or "free-economy"-oriented, are largely self-styled brokers on behalf of their masses; (2) that the governments consider themselves agencies of development; (3) that by "development" is meant almost exclusively "economic progress"; (4) that this is more or less in keeping with the contemporary Western model, for which progress also means basically economic and technological expansion and where intellectual and moral—that is, humanistic—values have sharply declined; (5) that in the East, including the Muslim world, the problem has become further compounded by (*a*) the fact that the new technology and its attendant phenomena are "imported" and are not organically related to the traditional cultures of these developing societies and (*b*) the fact that many thinkers in the preindependence period in these countries had popularized the slogan that the East is spiritualist while the West is materialist and that if the East merely exports some of its spirituality to the West and, in exchange, imports some technology from the West, all will be right with the world; (6) that the masses in these countries are uneducated, ignorant, and extremely conservative and do not meaningfully participate in their governments irrespective of whether they be rightist or leftist, dictatorial or democratic. They would like to possess the material goods that accrue from modern technology, but they will not easily give up their traditional way of life, particularly their negative work ethic. Consequently there is, in this respect at least, hardly any effective communication between their broker governments and themselves. Finally and most important, (7) this political, social, and moral situation is aggravated and made far more pernicious by the extremely low priority given to education because of the myopic vision of progress as being purely material. Since their independence, (*a*) education in these countries is basically a continuation of the colonial education, which essentially meant training petty government officials to serve the colonial rulers; it offers neither a real grounding in traditional culture nor a genuine training to exercise responsibility in a free modern society; (*b*) the education of the traditionalist religious institutions, unless adequately adjusted, is inevitably moribund and is, in any case, in fast decline, because (*c*) the new education in terms of the production of technological professionals (engineers, doctors, "scientists") has, to all appearances, irreversibly stolen the position of prestige formerly occupied by traditional education.

Although the above description generally applies to Muslim countries at present, this dismal state of affairs is somewhat relieved by the awareness, not altogether lacking in the more progressive of them, that the current situation cannot be allowed to continue and that education, to become more meaningful, has to be more effectively integrated with basic cultural values. It is interesting to note that, in the colonial period, several Muslim thinkers had been much more clear about educational issues: we saw in the previous chapter the strictures passed by Muḥammad Iqbāl, ʿAbduh, Zia Paša, and others both on the slavishly "modern" education pursued in these countries and also on the contemporary and fast-changing values of the West. All these people insisted that education, if it is to be worthy of its name, must have a goal, and that that goal is not simply identifiable with material progress, since this leads inherently to the diminution and distortion of the human being. Nor yet is it identifiable with the traditional education, since, being out of tune with the new siutation, it is no more than a hard, lifeless shell unless new life is infused into it. But after independence dawned, bringing with it the ideology of "planning for progress," this vision of the classical modernist was so ruthlessly blighted that its restoration, even if both the vision and will are there, is certainly not going to be an easy task.

I have given two reasons for the lack up to now of creative education among Muslim societies: first, a sort of passive and inept carrying on with the educational systems of the colonial period or, in the case of Turkey, a slavish imitation of the Western model; second, the fascination that the ideology of material progress exercised on the planners. This fascination was coupled with a blindness to the fact that technology cannot succeed at improving human society unless the mind of man changes—unless he is imbued with a new motivation. This can be done in Muslim societies only by linking it with some higher purpose and with a concretely formulated and stated goal. Had this been done, Islam could have been an extraordinarily powerful catalyst for progress; for relief of misery and alleviation of poverty and suffering are writ large into the Qur'ān and the Sunna of the Prophet.

But besides these two factors—and, I suspect, much stronger and deeper—was the fact that the modern-educated elite in these countries, particularly those groups that have been at the helm of affairs, have lacked the courage to face up to the situation and take the requisite measures to solve the problem. I have already hinted at the "soft" nature of these developing states, the reason for which is undoubtedly the vast gap between the ignorance and conservatism of the masses and the modernity (not *modernism,* of course!) of the ruling elites. Yet the only real measure that can bridge this yawning gap—education—is awarded a very low priority in the "planning strategies" of these nations, resulting in a dire lack of communication between the two and a lopsided "development." Although an undercurrent of suspicion endures between the two, the ruling elites are ever fearful of incurring the explicit hostility of the masses and therefore refuse to do anything unpopular, that is, undertake any tangible reform in those social sectors, including education, that are culturally sensitive. And without the counterpart of the "social" reform, the purely "economic" reform will not work. Even the great and powerful Atatürk could not reform traditional education. After attempting reform, even through personal Friday sermons from the pulpit for several years (from 1922 to 1928), he could "reform" religious education only by eliminating it altogether. This disparity between the governments (and their paraphernalia) and the masses that thwarted Atatürk's reform attempts remains the main obstacle to real progress in these countries.

But, as I have said, this current situation is not a stable one, for, to be sure, there is awareness in many minds of the incompatibility of the traditional with the modern, with varying degrees of perception and points of emphasis. Some "moderns" would like to eliminate the "religious" in favor of the secular as Atatürk did (although we shall soon learn something of what happened in post-Kemālist Turkey); others would prefer to keep the two separate, creating either two nations in a country or two minds in one individual. But by far the commonest strategy of the planners is to "mix" the two in a proportion that often suits one group at the expense of the other and that at any rate is too recent an experiment for its results to be predicted with confidence. I shall have something to say, however, by way of an interim assessment in the next chapter. For the time being I shall attend to sketching out these developments themselves in a sufficiently clear, though necessarily brief, outline.

Islam and Educational Reform: Turkey and Egypt

Perhaps the most spectacular development in Islamic education in contemporary Islam has occurred in Turkey,[1] where, after a quarter of a century's official total ban, it resurrected itself through sheer public pressure. Voices had been raised from different parts of the country complaining that, owing to the nonavailability of qualified personnel, the dead had sometimes to be buried without proper funeral services. At last, with the introduction of democracy (i.e., a multiparty system) in 1946, the Republican party (Atatürk's party) saw that the opposition party (the Democratic party) might successfully campaign on the issue of freedom of religious education. The Republican leader, Inönü, decided to undercut the opposition and established an imam–hatip school (school for training imāms and khatībs) in 1948. By 1949 the Faculty of Theology (Ilāhiyāt Fakültesi) was established within Ankara University. In the National Parliament much anxiety was expressed lest the new Faculty of Theology should once again help generate the rigidity and obscurantism of the old madrasas. The minister of national education replied that the proposed Faculty of Theology was a natural result of the reform processes set in motion by Atatürk and furthermore said:

> This idea is essentially of a nature that will put to rest our friends' anxieties. We are not of the opinion that the old Madrasa should be revived. . . . School and Madrasa, beginning with the Tanzimat, lived side by side for a hundred years and bred people who had two different types of mentality. This person with a two-fold mentality rolled through a whole century with an inner struggle. The Faculty of Divinity that we are about to establish will not work with this mentality. . . . The Faculty of Divinity will be established as a scientific body. . . . The Faculty of Divinity will be a torch of light like other scientific institutions.[2]

1. In the following pages of this chapter, I have decided to treat Egypt and Turkey together, not only because they represent cohesive societies, but also because in both the relationship between the ulema and the government is very intimate. Iran, Pakistan, and Indonesia will each be dealt with separately in order to bring out their peculiar situations before I generalize in the last chapter.

2. Ḥusayin Atay, "Islamic Education in Turkey," unpublished monograph, part of the University of Chicago research project, p. 210.

It is apparent that at this stage the imam-hatip schools and the Faculty of Theology were thought of as being quite separate from one another, since there is no mention of any idea of linking the two. The schools were to produce religious functionaries like imāms and khatībs, while the Faculty of Theology was to be the intellectual center for a scientific understanding (and interpretation?) of Islam. A decade later, in 1959, the idea of establishing higher Islamic institutes was mooted. With these institutes, the external structure is complete enough, but the curricula are still evolving. The curriculum of the Ankara Faculty of Theology, for example, was changed for a last time in 1976. At present (1977) there are 249 imam-hatip schools and eight higher Islamic institutes (with a four-year curriculum) throughout the country. At the university level, there is the Faculty of Theology at Ankara and the Faculty of Islamic sciences (Islam Ilimleri Fakültesi) at the Atatürk University in Erzerum established in 1971, each with a five-year undergraduate training course. And at the University of Istanbul, within its Faculty of Letters, there is an Institute of Islamic Studies.

It should be noted that students who enroll in imam-hatip schools (most of which are in the countryside) do not do so necessarily with the intention of pursuing a religious career: most of these schools are like ordinary schools where one gets the education to follow whatever profession one may wish to pursue later on. In many cases these are the only schools available to parents in the countryside, so they send their children there. Of course many parents also *prefer* to send their children to these schools because they offer instruction in the religion of Islam besides giving a basic education. It should also be noted that the buildings housing most of these schools, as well as those of the higher Islamic institutes, are constructed by local community effort, and only after their construction does the government hire teachers. This shows the real basis of the strength of Turkish Islam: it is part and parcel of that extraordinarily intense feeling of national being by which no concerned visitor can fail to be struck. It is quite an experience. When I visited a new higher Islamic institute building that was just receiving its finishing touches, a senior member of the committee that was responsible for its construction said to me, "Our community [i.e., *not* the government] has built it by its own effort; from this you can see how strong Islam is here; but from this you can also gauge how powerful Atatürk was, since despite this strength he was able to suppress it for a quarter of a century!"

Some measure of the change of mood will be gained from the speech, made in the National Parliament on the occasion of the passage of the law concerning the establishment of the Ankara Faculty of Theology, by the eccentric aesthetician of religion Ismail Hakki Baltacioğlu, an adviser of Atatürk on religious reform whom we met in the previous chapter. Among other things he said, "After fifty years I have come to the conviction, and I do not refrain from expressing it from this seat, viz. that if a man, after acquiring all cultures of ethics, aesthetics, and literature, does not receive religious education—I am not talking of a structured type of education to be imparted by the government—human personality cannot be complete."[3] Speaking of the first Faculty of Theology set up within Istanbul University by Atatürk in 1924 (where he himself was a professor) and of its subsequent closure, Baltacioğlu said, "We had made it into some kind of a faculty of sociology; but in the [proposed] faculty, the Islamic sciences will be the main subjects and [the] sociological . . . ancillary."[4]

The main problem before the newly instituted system of Islamic education was, of course, that of teachers. Most of the ulema of the older generation were dead, and those few who had survived were very old. Since some Islamic education had gone on privately both in the cities (even though wherever this was discovered, both teachers and students were punished by government authorities) and, on a larger scale, in the countryside, it was not difficult to find enough qualified people to teach lower grades in the schools; but teachers for the higher school grades were almost nonexistent. As I hinted above, this was the reason it took a decade (from 1948 to 1959) to set up higher Islamic institutes. But, in these circumstances, who would man the Faculty of Theology at Ankara? Apart from some surviving relics of the past generation (who would, in any case, not only be inadequate but could even harm the task envisaged for the new institution), who was there? It is clear that for disciplines like history and philosophy, if any professors could be found, they would be secular-educated—those who might have taken their degrees at Western universities and have had little to do

3. Ibid., p. 207.
4. Ibid.

with Islamic learning. The teaching of Arabic had been banned by the reforming zeal of Atatürk, hence the only link with Islam left was the Ottoman language and the Ottoman history and older sciences that had been enshrined in that language. These subjects were certainly cultivated by a few scholars, but they were actually Muslim *orientalists*—that is, they studied the Islamo-Turkish past historically and "objectively" but, by definition, without any reference to normative Islam, and hence without any real possibility of making a constructive or formative contribution to Islam in Turkey for the future. It was in fact, teachers of these two types that were appointed to the faculty in the first instance.

But, in course of time, better and more adequate *Islamic* scholars have been and will be forthcoming. The academic products of the first decade and a half are by no means to be ignored, since a great deal has been achieved by way of editions of old Turkish manuscripts and archives and translation; this work is nevertheless limited to the creation of historical materials. But now, after more than two decades and a half, one can meet, among the younger faculty members, people of learning and commitment who hold much promise for the future. Many of them know Arabic adequately, have obtained doctorates from abroad, and are personally and intellectually committed to Islam. Further, they not only are historians, but are concerned with certain central intellectual disciplines of Islam, theology and philosophy, and so on. The studies of the Qurʾān and Ḥadīth are yet far from adequate, and it is to be hoped that a breakthrough in these all-important subjects will come, a breakthrough that will be at once scientific and creative—that is, that will adequately meet the criteria of objective research and will, at the same time, reformulate or reinterpret the bases of Islamic thought and practice in such a way as to help fulfill the deepest aspirations of the Turkish nation.

The great sign of hope is the restlessness and remarkable upward mobility of intellectual life in the new educational adventure of Islam in Turkey. This mobility is an inherent quality of Turkish character and, of course, also accrues directly from the circumstance that Turkey is starting over with a clean slate after a deliberate and extended experiment with pure secular Westernization. In the next chapter I shall attempt to compare the situation with that in countries of long cumulative tradition without such a rupture—particularly Egypt—and try to establish the possible balance of advantage. In the meantime, one might feel justified in hoping that, when the minister of education made his aforementioned speech in Parliament in 1949, interpreting anew the Law of the Unification of Education of 1924 to the effect that the mental dualism of the century since the Tanzīmāt will not be allowed to grow again, and emphasized that the new institution will deal scientifically with Islamic research, he meant what I have taken it to mean: namely, that its research will meet the standards of sound scholarship but at the same time will be purposeful and formative—that it will be neither obscurantist, nor apologetic, nor yet Islamically colorless as is a purely "historical" or "objective" scholarship of orientalism. By the term "scientific," the first two seem to be categorically denied; but it shold not mean the third either, for in that case this research would be done not under the new meaning that has been given to the Law of the Unification of Education, but according to the old meaning, namely, that religion would be effectively kept out of national education. If *religion* is to be brought into and integrated with the national education, then this implies an interpretive, creative effort on the part of committed intellectuals so that religion not only is rescued from obscurantism and apologetics but helps make national life meaningful by giving it a new moral orientation. Certainly the actual developments appear to be going this way.

The Ankara and Erzerum departments have a similar curriculum, and both give degrees in two fields: in theology and philosophy and in Qur'ānic exegesis and Ḥadīth. I have remarked above that in my view the teaching of philosophy and social sciences or sociology has to be made larger and more sophisticated. Although some philosophy should be taught to all, as is already the case, a comprehensive and in-depth study of philosophy is particularly essential for those who graduate in the disciplines of Islamic theology and philosophy. The curriculum does emphasize Islamic philosophy in this connection, but a good grounding in general, and particularly modern, philosophy may be even more beneficial for a new interpretation of Islam than the systems of medieval Muslim philosophers like al-Fārābī and Ibn Sīnā. But it would be a mistake to think that Western philosophy is also colorless and "purely rational," since it is obviously the product of a definite cultural context. As for sociology or sociohistorical studies, these are extremely necessary for the most central disciplines of Islam—the Qur'ān and Ḥadīth and Islamic law. For unless the student knows the background of the Qur'ānic pronouncements, for example, it is *impossible* to understand their real import. I shall discuss this question of background further in the next chapter (as I have also outlined it in the Introduction); here I wish to say that, although some sociology and history are necessary for all students, their importance for the study of the Qur'ān, the Ḥadīth, and fiqh can hardly be exaggerated. Greater emphasis can be given to these subjects now that the curriculum has been expanded from four to five years.

I am dealing here with higher Islamic education, but of course it is clear that school education is the cornerstone for the quality of higher education. In the new Turkish Islamic education system, the bases seem very healthy from the beginning. The emphasis on Arabic is deservedly heavy and, as we shall see below, contrasts very favorably with the "modern" Pakistani system, for example, wherein Arabic is hardly adequately taught. I was told by a professor of Arabic who is writing Arabic textbooks for Turks that one hundred thousand Turks are learning Arabic. And, of course, the level is often high. In various Islamic schools and colleges in Turkey I gave lectures in Arabic, and several in the audience discussed questions with me in Arabic, a sight one will never see outside the Arab world, except to a limited extent in Indonesia.

However, as is to be expected, problems must and do arise for students who go to these schools but intend to pursue some career outside the Islamic field. Since the curriculum is to some extent necessarily deficient in non-Islamic or "secular" subjects compared with that of other public schools, graduates cannot enter colleges or universities without taking a further exam. This is quite all right, and, if the student is compensated by a good enough knowledge of Islam, it is worth while to sacrifice a year or so in order to compete with the generality of secular school students on their own ground. The public secular school system also gives some instruction in religion, but it is nominal. In fact, this is the major problem all over the Muslim countries that are trying to integrate a meaningful Islamic education with a full modern curriculum. Another alternative of limited scale that is tried in Indonesia is to hold Islamic education programs in the afternoons after the general secular school hours for those keen to pursue Islamic education in depth. There is no shortcut solution to the problem, and one of these alternatives is simply imposed. Islam is not—like, say, Christianity—a religion that is centered upon a dogma and an ethic; it includes wider fields of social relations and hence requires much more time. Christianity and Hinduism, for example, have had a longer history than Islam, but the literature of Islam covers a far more comprehensive field and has a far greater direct relationship to life than these religions.

In certain areas of modern knowledge, such as anthropology, sociology, and psychiatry, Turks have produced some first-rate material that has won international recognition, an achievement *no* other Muslim country can boast of, with the exception of Pakistan, which has produced a first-rate mathematical physicist who, however, has pursued all of his creative career in the West. An important quality that distinguishes Turks from citizens of other Muslim nations is that comparatively very few of their intellectuals choose to spend their lives abroad—undoubtedly a manifestation of the strong Turkish nationalist feeling spoken of above. In the Islamic field, however, Turkey's creativity is still awaited, since the reintroduction of Islamic sciences is very recent. What is certain is that Turkey has not been able to sell her secularism to the Muslim world at large. Secularism has undoubtedly made strong inroads in various ways, but there is no sign that state secularism will ever be espoused.

Whereas in Turkey the new phenomenon of religious education is the result of the upsurge of public opinion, in Egypt the entire reorganization, consolidation, and vast expansion of the massive al-Azhar is the handiwork of the government itself. The religious institution (the Presidency of Religious Affairs) and the religious educational system in Turkey are also under government tutelage; but the initiatives have been taken and continue to be taken there only by the people, and the government has basically reacted, sometimes at the suggestion, at other times at the demand, of certain ulema. In certain basic features, then, and indeed in ethos, al-Azhar and the modern Turkish system are in marked contrast. The latter has sprung up under its own steam and possesses a definite élan of its own and a certain powerful vigor, while the former is one gigantic organism subject to pressure from without and making necessary adjustments to it. In the vigorous Turkish phenomenon, much has been thrown up that is highly conservative, but by and large the new Turkish Islamic intellectuals are remarkably open and alert, less defensive, more appropriative, and less fearful of exposure to outside ideas. At al-Azhar, by contrast, the nucleus of Islamic learning, and particularly the theological college, is relatively unchanged, despite massive changes at its outskirts in the recently established colleges of agriculture, medicine, and engineering. Since Islamic law was never abrogated in Egypt as it was in Turkey, al-Azhar, in its College of Law, may be able to bring about some real synthesis in this all-important field, although the internal intellectual and spiritual life of al-Azhar is extremely ponderous. There is no doubt that a certain amount of slowness in pace, that is, a certain amount of conservatism, is necessary for an integrated continuity, but one sometimes wonders and indeed fears if an institution like al-Azhar, even if it does want to move, can really advance at a meaningful speed or whether it is not like a great glacier that, although it grows huge by attracting all sorts of extraneous materials through its sheer size, slowly melts away leaving only a trail of debris.

Al-Azhar is an official institution and, as with all Islamic official institutions of the past centuries, although its organization changes, it more or less stays put in its intellectual-spiritual stance. It is—to use that word with all its difficulties in an Islamic context—the "orthodoxy." But changes in Islamic "orthodoxy" have always come about by a cumulative pressure that continues to build up outside its nucleus, and when a critical mass is reached the nucleus "re-forms" itself. It is not, therefore, surprising that al-Azhar moves very slowly. What is perhaps surprising is that there is so little pressure built around it. The other kind of pressure that it is subject to is, as I have said, government pressure, which may go in the right or the wrong direction but is, in any case, not the kind I have spoken about here, which brings a kind of "re-formation" (not reformation), that is, a reconstitution of the inner nucleus, and which also results in a rearrangement of its inner intellectual and spiritual factors, as has happened, for example, through the successive influences of al-Ghazālī, Ibn Taymiya, and the "Wahhābīs"—and, of course, through Islamic modernism.

The modernization of of al-Azhar had been begun by certain ulema in the nineteenth century, the most prominent of them being Muḥammad ʿAbduh. But its effects were felt in the fields of reorganization, examination systems, and introduction of new subjects—apart from a general leavening of ideas both in and outside al-Azhar—rather than in the content of the nuclear Islamic sciences such as theology and philosophy. ʿAbduh had certainly written an influential treatise on theology, the *Risālat al-Tawḥīd,* restating some of the fundamental theses of medieval Sunni kalām with new emphasis and reviving a Muʿtazilite type of rationalism, for example, on the question of human free will. But, although the work was good enough for its times, ʿAbduh was basically a traditionally educated ʿālim and can hardly be called a modern-educated man. After him there have been occasional pebbles thrown into the pond, causing some stir but hardly any big waves, let alone a revolution. ʿAbd al-Mutaʿāl al-Ṣaʿīdī contended in his book on the history of reform in al-Azhar[5] that the education imparted at al-Azhar could not breed mujtahids—that is, those who would have the capability and the desire to engage in new thinking on the various aspects of Islam, a thesis that seems to me to be a truism. Khālid Muḥammad Khālid in his *Min Hunā Nabdaʾ*[6] did the same in stronger terms and stirred up a vehement response. But none of these works forced the authorities of al-Azhar to modify the content of their Islamic teaching. The reasons are not far to seek. The fact is that al-Azhar represents the late medieval body of Islamic thought with certain new and minor modifications. People who criticize al-Azhar take as their point of departure the existing state of affairs—a state of affairs that carries within it the weight of long centuries of cumulative solidification. What is true of al-Azhar is true of all long, settled traditions in all religions. I am singling out al-Azhar in the case of Islam because it represents par excellence not only a long, settled, and solidified tradition but a massive one as well.

Now, whoever chooses to criticize such an institution *at its present point* does so by first implicitly accepting the entire solidified tradition as it has grown through the centuries and then advising certain changes or adjustments that therefore, in the nature of the case, must have only minor impact. But it is here that the real import of my chapter 1 is thrown into bold relief.

5. ʿAbd al-Mutaʿāl al-Ṣaʿīdī, *Taʾrīkh al-Iṣlāḥ fiʾl-Azhar* (Cairo: Maṭbaʿah Iʿtimād, 1951).

6. Khālid Muḥammad Khālid, *Min Hunā Nabdaʾ* [From here we start] (Cairo: Muʾassasah al-Khānjī, 1963).

For if that chapter tried to prove anything and left a lesson for reform, it was that the genesis and development of the whole Islamic tradition—the way the Qurʾān and the Sunna of the Prophet were approached, treated, and interpreted—was only one possible alternative among those available, which was chosen and then developed. As the quotation from al-Shāṭibī in chapter 1 might enable us to understand today, after the first few generations the interpretation of the Qurʾān and the Sunna was done *not* as an integrated whole, but as so many different pieces and parcels. The principle of analogy also did not prove as effective and beneficial as it might have, because it was applied after examining the two Islamic sources in a discrete and piecemeal manner, rather than after creating a unity out of the whole message and then deducing laws and norms of behavior from it. It is this fresh look *not at the present point of time at which, for example, al-Azhar is situated but at the initial point of the formulation of the central Islamic disciplines of law and theology* that can yield far-reaching results for Islamic progress.

But this activity cannot be done within al-Azhar, nor indeed ought al-Azhar, for reasons given above, to be the locus for this. It is outside of the official establishment that a fresh taking stock of the growth of the tradition can and must take place. And should this trend grow and reach a critical mass, it will then inevitably find a slow but sure response from the establishment; this is, as I have argued briefly above (and also in my previous book),[7] the way the "re-formation" of the orthodoxy has proceeded in the past. Al-Azhar has indeed responded well to calls for certain reforms before; but as an establishment it has its own dynamics. In the preceding chapter we saw the series of developments that took place at al-Azhar up to the laws of 1930 and 1939 that created the three faculties at the university in theology, Islamic law (Sharīʿa), and Arabic studies.

The most radical changes brought about since then were in the 1960s. In 1961 a law was enacted to institute as part of al-Azhar University a school of medicine, a school of agriculture, and a school of engineering. This huge change was basically necessitated by the fact that the vastly increased number of students at al-Azhar could not compete with products of the general system of education; these colleges then were aimed primarily

7. Fazlur Rahman, *Islam*, new ed. (Chicago: University of Chicago Press, 1979), chap. 6.

at solving this difficulty. But another tangible benefit was seen in the fact that a worthwhile class of professionals (doctors, engineers, agriculturists) would be created with a really solid knowledge of Islam as compared with the products of the general system, who have had no more than a smattering of religious knowledge. This is undoubtedly an extremely important development and, from a religious point of view, should have far-reaching effects on the texture of Egyptian social life. This development also has important implications for social change: the introduction of nurses in the teaching hospital and the breakdown of total sex segregation.

In 1962 a women's college was also set up within the al-Azhar complex, which has recently become a university (within al-Azhar) with a medical school of its own. These are surely, from a sociological point of view, stunning changes that are totally unparalleled in any other institution of Islamic learning in the Muslim world. The net effect of all these measures, as I have just said, would be to give a strong religious character to the society as large. Indeed, through a very large number of foreign students whom it was able to attract after a sustained financial effort in the 1950s, the influence of al-Azhar (and of course Egypt) is reaching far beyond the Egyptian borders (although its effect in the South Asian subcontinent appears to be minimal so far). It also frequently sends out missions and other personnel for community work abroad, particularly now in Western countries.

A question, however, that must be raised once again is: With all this huge machine and with all this vast influence, is Islamic teaching qualitatively faring better at al-Azhar than in other smaller institutions in the Muslim world? Is it producing better scholars, not only with greater commitment to Islam, but also with sharper, clearer, and more profound minds? May it not be that it is so fortunately placed, particularly financially, that its security tends to create a placidity and a lack of the intellectual and spiritual challenge and ferment that is absolutely essential for intellectual and spiritual progress? From the intellectual performance of its products to date one cannot be highly impressed; there is perhaps still too much emphasis on "acquisition of knowledge"—that is, learning a more or less static body of facts—than on creativity, which cannot come about without a disturbance of the mind and an intellectual adventuresomeness. But even if it is a question of "learning" facts rather than thinking creatively, what facts does one learn, how does one order them, and what values are attached to them?

The list of subjects taught is very comprehensive; it is more or less like the list of subjects of the Faculty of Theology at Ankara, for example. There are not just the sciences of Qur'ān commentary, Ḥadīth, kalām, and such, but social sciences, psychology, comparative religion, and so forth. If they are taught well, with a critical-analytical approach, there is no reason a creative thought movement should not start sooner or later, except for the consideration I mentioned earlier, namely, the weight of history and al-Azhar's monopoly of Islamic education in Egypt. In addition, the approach seems to be apologetic. It is perhaps not without interest that there recurs a subject in the al-Azhar curriculum titled "defense of the Qur'ān against Western attacks." In Ḥadīth such a "defense" may be understandable, since several prominent Western scholars have gravely doubted the authenticity of much of the Ḥadīth, but what can such a defense of the Qur'ān mean? No Western scholar of any importance has really created any doubt about the integrity and authenticity of the Qur'ānic text except that some orientalists have suggested, for example, that certain suras date from a period before Muḥammad's actual calling as Prophet (a strange idea in itself, indeed), and certainly there is Richard Bell's eccentric theory about the continuous revision of the Qur'ān by the Prophet (under divine direction!). But these and similar theories—that of John Wansbrough, for example (whose theses are, however, stillborn)—can have very little influence on Western scholarship itself, and there is little doubt that the generality of Western scholars do not doubt the authenticity of the Qur'ānic text. Indeed, on this issue certain early medieval extremist Shīʿī views have been much more dangerous. It would be much more profitable for constructive Qur'ān studies if the al-Azhar ulema were to study the Qur'ān and the development and interconnection of its ideas in a more scholarly manner that would elucidate its élan, its goals, and its values and principles. (It is also interesting that this "defense" of the Qur'ān does not appear in Turkish syllabi.) A very encouraging development is the introduction of "secular" law (*qānūn*) into the Faculty of Sharīʿa. Besides producing lawyers who combine knowledge of both kinds of law, this should result, in course of time, in an integration or synthesis of the two traditions. And, as we shall see, the situation of al-Azhar ulema is far more advanced than, for example, that of the ulema of Pakistan, for whom even the question of what non-Muslim scholars have written on the various aspects of Islam has not yet arisen.

Not only is al-Azhar one huge monopolistic organization, but it is dependent upon government patronage. The two facts are, of course, allied. This is not the place to attempt an analysis of the situation, but there is no doubt that this dependence stabilizes their mutual relationships. Not only is it easier for al-Azhar to rely on government support for its necessary programs that the government thinks are useful, and hence to monopolize Islam in a way that is impossible for institutions in other countries, but equally important, if not more important, is the fact that the government can ensure compliance with or elimination of active opposition against such of its intentions and programs as may be religiously sensitive. It is obvious that this will inculcate a greater sense of responsibility in the religious leadership and lessen the risk of the wild and reckless denunciations of government policies that religious leaders in other countries sometimes make. On the other hand, it is equally clear that this situation can dull not only brains but consciences as well, and this, if it goes beyond a certain point, can make self-defeating the entire purpose of a religious leadership as watchmen of the moral sensibilities and behavior of the community and its political leadership.

The Case of Iran

Whereas Islamic education in Turkey is supported by the government but based on the demand of the people and on their contributions, and whereas in Egypt it is financed and dominated by the government and concentrated in the single massive umbrella institution of al-Azhar, the situation in Iran is different from both. The ulema institution is "free" there and is basically supported by merchants and people at large, with some contribution from the Organization of Awqāf. While through the laws of 1907, 1911, 1930, and 1934 the governments of Iran have sought to bring the Islamic educational system under their control in organization and curriculum, they have succeeded very little. In the meantime the ulema of Iran (whether or not, as several Western scholars believe—without, I think, requisite evidence—in the eyes of the Shīʿī ulema all "mundane" governments in the absence of the infallible imām are ab initio illegitimate) have been politically very powerful, particularly since the latter half of the nineteenth century, on the basis of wide public support against their governments on many issues. It appears to me, however, that the ulema were able to arouse the public and exercise massive political power against the government not because the people saw the government as illegitimate, but because these issues involved national freedom and the government's acts were seen to weaken national independence in the face of foreign interference. This was the case with the Tobacco Concessions given to the British in the later years of the nineteenth century, and this was also the case with the fatwās issued for the necessity of nationalizing the Anglo-Iranian Oil Company in the late 1940s and early 1950s. Finally, this must explain—only this time foreign interference was seen not only in the political and economic field but equally sharply in the cultural field—the Khomeinī revolution of 1979. When, however, the government has a good cause and the ulema oppose it, the government can get away with ruthless acts to carry through its policy: witness the opposition of the ulema to the projected land reforms of the shāh in the late 1950s and early 1960s and the shāh's devastating firing of the ulema in 1963.

But although the religious establishment had been very considerably weakened during the past few decades in Iran, the effective public role of the ulema had on principle not been destroyed because their public clientele was still available to them. It is, however, a moot question whether the ulema's patronage and control by the government or their "free" status makes for greater progress and modernization. Judging from the experience of Iran and Pakistan and contrasting it with that of, say, Egypt, it seems that the ulema, without effective government guidance and direction—if not outright control—are unable to make the necessary progress. First of all, the traditional learning of the ulema makes them conservative, and the rise of a progressive reformer among their own ranks is rare indeed. But, second, it is also questionable whether they are "free" when they are not under government control or supervision. For in that case it becomes difficult for them to rise above the mentality of the masses or merchants who support them and who are on the whole highly conservative and unenlightened. My own experience in Pakistan has led me to this view; and the evidence in Shahrough Akhavi's excellent monograph on Islamic education in Iran confirms this point.[8] In general this point can be deduced by necessary logic, for unless the masses become relatively enlightened in a "free" system of education, the level of education cannot rise. After all, this has been one of the two important reasons why the governments have taken over general education, the other being the cost of education, which is beyond the range of private hands. It is therefore fruitless to expect that a privately financed system of education, Islamic or "secular," can succeed in producing men of learning who would be solid and creative while its financial supporters remain unenlightened.

However, government control or intervention, unless exercised with an enlightened head and a sincere heart, can be harmful not only to the morale of the religious leadership but even to the substance of education itself. The Iranian law of 1934, for example, thinned down the curriculum of Islamic education (to be administered during a twelve-year span) so much that the substance of instruction in terms of material to be studied was considerably less than matriculation standard, which is laughable. As Akhavi points out in the aforementioned work,[9] this particular syllabus totally removed the philosophical disciplines (*ḥikmat*), which had been the pride of Iranian intellectualism through the centuries, along with several other areas, from the syllabus and put in its place elementary accounting and astronomy—not modern, but classical! Nobody who went through this curriculum could be called an ʿālim unless it was intended as a term of ridicule. It is no wonder then that the madrasas continued to teach additional works and areas of study. The 1934 syllabus also included certain subjects that had fallen into disuse for some time in the madrasas—Qurʾān commentary, history, and biographical literature on Ḥadīth transmitters, besides making Islamic law the focal point of education.

The relatively high level of an unbroken philosophical tradition in Iran has kept the intellectual standards relatively high, resulting, at least in religiophilosophical circles, in the inculcation

8. Shahrough Akhavi, *Religion and Politics in Contemporary Iran* (Albany: State University of New York Press, 1980). This study was a part of the aforementioned University of Chicago project.

9. Ibid., pp. 51 ff.

of a critical spirit for a long time virtually unknown in the Sunni countries. This relatively free intellectualism has also entered into the area of the theory of law (*uṣūl al-fiqh*), where, toward the end of the seventeenth century and in the early eighteenth century, the "intellectualist" school of thought (the Uṣūlīs) won a decisive victory over the approach of the strict "traditionalists" (Akhbārīs) in legal theory. Indeed, it would be true to say of many Persian intellectuals that a rather free and critical intellectualism, resulting from a predilection for philosophy, has become a hallmark of Iranian Shīʿī Islam in contradistinction to Sunni Islam. However, this intellectualism has had little effect on the teaching of law itself, that is, the substantive provisions of law as distinguished from legal theory; in fact, the former is as traditional as it can be and consists of learning certain medieval texts by rote. It is one of the remarkable phenomena in Islam that all rationalist groups, like the Muʿtazila and the philosophical Shīʿa, who have exercised their intellectualism with astonishing freedom, have fallen in line with tradition on practical matters, keeping intellectual and practical aspects of life somehow in watertight compartments: the *ijmāʿ*, or *past consensus,* has effectively prevented legal *ijtihād,* or new thinking on legal matters. This, of course, does not mean that changes do not occur at all in practical life, but they happen more by a pragmatic and instinctive adjustment than through intellectually considered opinion, which seems to have little direct relationship with practical issues and appears to be undertaken for its own sake and purely for an enjoyment of the abstract. A striking case of this kind of mental dualism is Āyatullāh Khomeinī, the postrevolutionary ruler of Iran.

In 1960 there appeared a movement against this fiqh-oriented education in the form of a society called "the Association for a Religious Monthly," the name of the monthly being *Guftār-i-Māh* (*Monthly Speeches*). Several younger ulema from the Qum establishment joined it, particularly certain students of Burūjirdī (who was, until his death in 1961, "the absolute authority in religion"—marjiʿ-i-taqlīd-i-muṭlaq). The views of this reformist group were set forth in the aforementioned monthly as well as in a volume essentially devoted to the question of marjiʿ-i-taqlīd, or religious authority, entitled, "*Baḥs-i Dar Bāreh-yi Marjiʿiyat wa Rūḥāniyat*" (*Investigation concerning Religious Authority and Religious Leadership*). The main demands of this group were the creation of an autonomous financial organization and the setting up of a council of religious authority (rather than one or more individuals) to issue authoritative opinions on religious issues, to emphasize ethics, theology, and philosophy instead of law in the curriculum, and, in order to implement Islam as a total way of life, to produce people who could perform true ijtihād or original thinking in matters that demand new solutions. The main personality in this movement was Murtazā Muṭahharī, a professor in the Faculty of Theology of Tehran University (which, compared with the Faculty of Theology of Ankara University, is much more oriented toward traditional Islamic sciences, including philosophy).

The leaders of this society, therefore, challenged the capability of the existing ulema to lead the Iranian masses in general and the new youth in particular and interpreted the Qur'ānic exhortation "to command good and forbid evil" as devolving upon the community as a whole and not as restricted to the ulema: only in this way could Islamic demands be satisfied and the country's national aspirations of progress and independence from the West be fulfilled. While the reformers insisted on strengthening Islam and Islamic education, their program naturally involved changes that seemed to the conservative ulema too drastic. Furthermore, the government itself could hardly be expected to accept a reform that would not only create an autonomous rival to it but could endanger its very existence, if the Shūrā-yi-Fatwā's function would be absolutist and not merely, as is the case with Pakistan's Islamic Advisory Council, advisory to the government. Yet the reformists appear to have been basically sincere people who did not envisage harm to the state; rather, in order to legitimize the state in religious terms, they insisted on implementing the concept of "delegation" of the state powers from God, the Prophet, and the imāms (in contradistinction to the more democratic way that, for example, the Constitution of Pakistan has taken, namely, the delegation of such powers from God to the people and through the people to the state). In 1963, amid the furor and tragic events over the land reforms, the government suppressed the society and closed down its monthly, and the most important living 'ālim, Khomeinī, was exiled.

Yet, almost in continuity with this movement, there appeared a still more radical phenomenon known as the "Ḥusayniya Irshād," or "the Guidance of Ḥusayn." The man who attracted the limelight in this new group was ʿAlī Sharīʿatī, who himself combined a traditional education with a doctoral degree in sociology from the Sorbonne. Sharīʿatī made a strong call for the religious utopia of the Shīʿī ulema, including the imāms, to come down to earth, a call in which he was both preceded and joined by the engineer of thermodynamics Bāzargān, the first prime minister of postrevolutionary Iran. He made an explicit plea for the Shīʿa to consolidate with the larger Sunni community and its leadership, claiming that the Safavids distorted the Shīʿa perspectives for their own interests and that the Shīʿī "awaiting" the return of the hidden imām had been turned into something passive and negative vis-à-vis the positive and action-oriented principles of Islam. His message called for the creation of a social moral awareness on the part of the community at large and for "political activism." Although the younger generation, both lay-educated people and madrasa students, responded warmly—indeed, enthusiastically—to his call, both the older conservative ulema and the government resented his proposed drastic measures to "awaken" Muslim masses against indigenous and foreign (Western) exploiters, and one by one his own colleagues left him. After seven years of successful experimentation with this kind of modernization through lectures and books, the Ḥusayniya Irshād of Sharīʿatī was closed down, and he himself was sent to jail. He was subsequently exiled and died suddenly in London in June 1977, where he is generally believed to have been assassinated by the ex-shāh's agents. The salient feature of Sharīʿatī's program, which claimed to derive sociologicohistorical principles from the Qurʾān, but which also applied modern sociologicohistorical principles to the interpretation of the Qurʾān, was a massive research effort. He sought to establish a new Islamic education that would be consonant with his own approach to understanding the Qurʾān and drastically different from the traditional Islamic approach, whose representatives he accused of "making Islam stand on its head." How could they, in turn, suffer being made to stand upon *their* heads? His influence upon the younger generation of students is profound and is likely to reassert itself, although at present Khomeinī's power is supreme.

What Happened to Pakistan?

In the face of the ideological background struggle for Pakistan, it might be expected that a system of education would have evolved there, sooner rather than later, that would be the bearer of her ideology, that her ideology, that is, Islam, would be interpreted and worked out in enough detail to inform all spheres of her life, and that this ideological elaboration would be true to Islamic ideals, yet sufficiently progressive to enable necessary modernization. The statements of Muḥammad Iqbāl, the spiritual father of Pakistan, given in the preceding chapter, severely criticizing both traditional and modern lay (British) systems of education, would be expected to generate an effective movement for a synthesis of the old and the new. That at least this feeling of urgency was present in the minds of the creators of Pakistan is shown by the fact that soon after 16 August 1947 the Qāʾid-i-Aʿẓam, Muḥammad ʿAlī Jinnah, said to the educationists, in a social function arranged for the members of the Constituent Assembly, "Now that we have got our own state, it is up to you to establish a viable, productive and sound system of education suited to our needs. It should reflect our history and our national ideals."[10] Further, despite the largest migration of people in known human history, and the problems accompanying it—including the greatest slaughter of humans in history—the Pakistan government summoned an Education Conference on 27 November 1947 where the minister of education, Fazlur Rahman, stated: "It is, therefore, a matter of profound satisfaction to me as it must be to you, that we have now before us the opportunity of reorienting our entire educational policy to correspond closely with the needs of the times and to reflect the ideals for which Pakistan as an Islamic state stands. This is a great, indeed, a unique opportunity but even greater is the magnitude of the task which it imposes upon us."[11] In this address, great emphasis was laid on the inculcation of moral ideals through education.

One would think that Iqbāl himself was speaking, so complete was the identity of views and intensity of feeling on this issue between the pre-Pakistan and immediately post-Pakistan days. And yet, about three decades later, I. H. Qureshī (d. 1981), the

10. Ishtiāq Ḥusain Qureshī, *Education in Pakistan* (Karachi: Maʿaref, 1975), p. 27.

11. Ibid., p. 29.

veteran educator and educationist who lived through it all, tells us: "Our secular educated elite is the most spineless, the most unscrupulous and the most mercenary in the world. . . . What has gone wrong during this quarter of a century that has eaten into the vitals of our society and the grit of its leaders except the continuation of a faulty, aimless, and diseased system of education that has bred no social virtues, no depth of feeling, no sense of responsibility—nothing except selfishness, corruption and cowardly lack of initiative and courage?"[12] A little further on, Qureshī continues, "They [the leaders of traditional education] have neglected modern knowledge to an extent that there is no scope left for a dialogue between those who have received a modern education and the graduates of the seminaries. . . . The seminaries are doing useful [!] work in the preservation of the classical theological learning and providing ill-paid, ill-educated and ill-informed imams of the mosques. It is quite obvious that such education cannot help the growth of religious consciousness."[13]

My task here is to try to explain the gap between the claims and expectations of 1947 and the agonizing admission of failure of 1975, and the nature of the trends and developments that fill this gap. It is clear that at the time of its inception Pakistan's leaders were generally highly liberal, and, while they wanted to inform their educational system with an Islamic orientation, this Islamic orientation, in their eyes, was not only tolerant but positively liberal. This fact is primarily attributable to their exposure to British education. The speeches of Fazlur Rahman, the first education minister, are a clear testimony to this.[14] Indeed, at the first Education Conference, referred to above, the Right Reverend G. D. Barnes, Anglican bishop of Lahore, was assured enough of the liberal attitude of Pakistan to approve emphatically the resolution that called for basing education in Pakistan on Islamic principles. Nevertheless, from its very genesis, Pakistan was the victim of a widespread lack of sympathy, indeed even large-scale antipathetic propaganda in some of the largest and most influential nations of the world. That an officially atheistic Russia would have considered an Islamic state like Pakistan

12. Ibid., pp. 119 ff.
13. Ibid., p. 117.
14. Fazlur Rahman [Minister of Education, Pakistan, 1947–57], *The New Education in the Making in Pakistan* (London: Cassell, 1953).

anathema is obvious; but the situation in America was hardly better, since Americans' experience of state secularism made them utterly ill-attuned to a country like Pakistan (notwithstanding Israel!). Whatever amity did develop later between Pakistan and the United States was at the level of the United States administration and was based on politicomilitary considerations; at the level of public opinion the attitude continued to be more antipathetic than even apathetic, thanks mainly to public propagandists like the public (information) media.

Much more important than whatever happened to Pakistan abroad, however, was what the Pakistanis did to themselves. First of all we notice an air of placidity on the very serious issues that the Education Conference of 1947 tried to tackle. Except for passing resolutions (and that these were carried unanimously, including the leaders of religious minorities, is an important achievement), nothing was done in terms of further action. No commission or committee was set up to further deliberate on this extremely vital matter and to make concrete recommendations. It seems as though the leaders considered said as good as done. Indeed, although Pakistan found in various fields of activity many a devoted worker whose enthusiasm helped this young and fragile nation survive the pangs of its birth, the atmosphere in general was rather one of euphoria than of facing a grave challenge. The achievement of Pakistan was in effect regarded as the end of the struggle. The result was that the Islamic orientation of education became an empty slogan.

This situation was undoubtedly perpetuated and even aggravated by the attitude of most of the higher echelons of the bureaucracy, who had been trained in British days to collect revenues and keep law and order. To develop the country and particularly to develop it on Islamic bases had been none of their concern, and it could not be expected that they would undergo so radical a change. A number of them were intensely attached to Islam, but many were literally frightened that insistence upon Islamic education might mean that the old-fashioned madrasa products would try to take over education. Therefore, though they could not expunge Islam from the official educational language, it was in fact no more than a platitude. I distinctly remember that in 1964, when the Second Five-Year Plan was on the anvil, I also received an invitation from the planners of education, along with vice-chancellors of universities and other educationists, to discuss the draft of the education plan. This draft began with the ritualistic statement to the effect that all education must be permeated with the values of Islam, but in the whole body of the draft up to the very end nothing Islamic was ever mentioned. When I asked a question about this matter, the chairman of the committee made a note in his book, but there is no doubt in my mind that he thought I was asking a rather absurd question.

If the government were serious about Islamic education, that is, about instituting a system of education that could, in a decade or so, produce the kind of person who might be able not only to help teach Islamic demands to the new society but also to spell out Islamic imperatives for state policies in view of the claims of Pakistan to be an "ideological" state, then one of several ways could be followed, or all of them could be followed simultaneously. After all, Pakistan had few engineers to start with but within a decade was able to produce several crops of engineers who could build roads and bridges. Why did Pakistan totally fail to produce equivalent persons in the Islamic field? This is our basic problem, and this we must answer as satisfactorily as possible. Let it be conceded that the analogy between education in Islam and, say, engineering is not quite strict: for one thing, engineering is a "skill" that is acquired through well-defined methods of teaching, whereas Islam pertains to the realm of thought and beliefs and is concerned not so much with "skills"—even though these are absolutely essential—as with the quality of mind and value orientations. Second, such professional skills as did not exist in Pakistani institutions—for example, nuclear technology—could be acquired from abroad, in Europe or America; but Islamic thought or, rather, the capacity for original Islamic thought, could not be acquired by Pakistanis either in a Western country or in a Muslim one. In Egypt, the leading country for Islamic studies, Islamic thought is hardly better than in Pakistan; for the impressive but ponderous al-Azhar, as it is, seems hardly capable of generating such original thought. But then Islam does not play the kind of role in Egypt that it was expected or assumed to play in Pakistan. Yet these obvious facts should have been foreseen before the creation of Pakistan, or at least soon thereafter. And it is not inconceivable that, even by making a new beginning, a system could have been gradually evolved that could do justice to the kind of situation Pakistan was in. Some attempts were indeed made, as we shall see; but partly through the paucity of existing human materials and largely through grievous misconceptions about what Islamic studies should mean *for Pakistan,* these attempts have proved fruitless.

One alternative was to take the existing madrasas and to persuade—by goodwill and support—as many of them as possible to adjust their curricula and methods of teaching in such a way as to streamline them into the general system of education while preserving their specialist nature. It is true that perhaps most ulema were suspicious of the modernist ruling elite and its sincerity toward Islam, but the point is that these suspicions were largely correct. If the ruling elite had been sincere, it could have done much to persuade many traditional madrasas to change their ways. As I pointed out toward the end of the first chapter, madrasas and ulema greatly increased in number after the creation of the Pakistani state. But because of the essential insincerity of the rulers, not only could these resources not be harnessed for developing Islamic education, but ill will between the government and the madrasas, which existed from the first day of the state of Pakistan, increased as time passed. Further, because of the real or imagined power and influence of these institutions and their personnel over the public, the ruling modernist was afraid of them, and this fear greatly hampered the sorely needed task of social modernization. The classic example of this hypocritical attitude is represented by the education policy announced by the government of the late Z. A. Bhutto in early 1972, which simply declared that "so far as private religious educational institutions are concerned the status quo will be maintained." It is quite clear that the fact that these institutions were private was used as a mere pretext by successive governments, since, in a state that claims to be based upon the ideology of Islam, what sense does it make to have private institutions that can deal with Islam as they choose? Can Russia or China allow private institutions to interpret communism as they like? There is, of course, the question of democratic processes, and this is why I contend here that, if the governments had used goodwill and persuasion, many of these institutions would have radically improved by now—three decades is not a short span of time. Suppose a private institution is established today in Pakistan with the purpose of teaching, say, Marxism. Will Pakistani authorities remain indifferent to it? The only time the Pakistani government decided to face this problem honestly was the educational policy statement issued by Air Marshal Muḥammad Nūr Khān during his very brief tenure as minister of education in the summer of 1969 during General Yaḥyā Khān's regime; but Nūr Khān was quickly removed from his post!

Madrasas, after partition, proliferated in Pakistan, even more so after 1960, and a good many of them are to be found in medium-sized towns, to the extent that one can speak of a new intelligentsia, even in the countryside, that has been influenced by them. This means that orthodox Islam, which was previously found almost exclusively in the cities, has extended itself to the countryside, where in the past Sufi Islam—often in its superstitious and corrupt forms—had prevailed. There is thus a sort of "religious progress" in the countryside and towns, but the same orthodox Islam in the cities represents a late medieval form of conservatism. These madrasas are largely modeled on Deoband, whose syllabus I discussed in chapter 1. It is, however, important to note that whereas, before partition, different variations of religious education appeared to attempt to fill this gap between the medieval Deoband and the modern Aligarh—the Nadwat al-ʿUlamā', for example—no such significant variant has appeared in Pakistan. The madrasas have stayed put where they were in 1947, except that some elementary English is being taught now among the more advanced of them. That no improved version of a madrasa has appeared in the past three decades is a comment on the state of affairs of the traditional Islamic education in Pakistan bemoaned so strongly by Ishtiāq Ḥusain Qureshī in the quotation cited above.

A very important Islamic phenomenon in the private sector, besides the madrasas, is of course the Jamāʿat-i-Islāmī. The Jamāʿat has been politically and socially active since the early forties, but its performance from the perspective of the present all-important problem of Islamic education has been not merely inadequate, but positively harmful. Not only have its leaders not developed any educational institutions of their own in the Islamic field, but at the same time, by proclaiming themselves the representatives par excellence of Islam before the nation, they have successfully impeded the growth of progressive Islamic education in the private sector. One would not, in fact, be wrong in saying that the nonexistence of any improved version of Islamic education is directly attributable to the Jamāʿat. The reason is not far to seek. The new change of attitude toward Islam generated by Iqbāl and other lesser figures that turned the young generation away from the traditional ulema (the essence of this change—from which had directly emerged the idea of the Islamic state—being that Islam is the total way of life and is not limited to the "five pillars" to which the Islam of the ulema had become practically restricted) had been imbibed by Mawdūdī (d. 1979), the founder and leader of the Jamāʿat-i-Islāmī. Now Mawdūdī, though not an ʿālim, was nevertheless a self-taught man of considerable intelligence and had sufficient knowledge of Arabic to have access to the classical Arabic literature of Islam. He was by no means an accurate or a profound scholar, but he was undoubtedly like a fresh wind in the stifling Islamic atmosphere created by the traditional madrasas, and he represented a definite advance over the ulema in that he had a working knowledge of English and read some works of Western writers. The lay-educated youth, fired by Iqbāl's message, became an almost automatic clientele of Mawdūdī. But Mawdūdī displays nowhere the larger and more profound vision of Islam's role in the world. Being a journalist rather than a serious scholar, he wrote at great speed and with resultant superficiality in order to feed his eager young readers—and he wrote incessantly. He founded no educational institution and never suggested any syllabus for a reformed Islamic education. If this kind of development had taken place, his followers, through an enlightened and serious Islamic education, would have naturally become more independent-minded and could have led the way to the establishment of new educational institutions. But not one of Mawdūdī's followers ever became a serious student of Islam, the result being that, for the faithful, Mawdūdī's statements represented the last word on Islam—no matter how much and how blatantly he contradicted himself from time to time on such basic issues as economic policy or political theory.

Thus the well-meaning young enthusiast of Islam became a prisoner of one man's ideas. This is indeed a basic characteristic of such groups as the Jamāʿat and the Muslim Brotherhood, although members of the latter are in certain important respects better and more amenable to further development. Their attitude has been largely deliberately anti-intellectual, their reasoning being that Islam is really a "simple" and "clear-cut" affair, that the Prophet was never the center of an intellectual movement but rather headed a moral-practical movement, and that the ulema and Sufis, because of their vested interests, have made it complicated and have buried it under debris. The argument is both appealing enough and true enough, and yet in the form in which it is fed to the faithful it is highly fallacious and dangerous. For the unfolding of the Qurʾān and the Prophet's activity took approximately twenty-three years, and, because fourteen centuries have elapsed since that time, the problem inevitably arises of *understanding* what the Qurʾānic message and the protracted struggle of the Prophet were about and what they aimed at achieving—which is by no means a simple affair. Further, complications have occurred in the development of what is called the Prophet's Sunna, on which a great many historic Islamic institutions and laws have been based or rationalized. The study of all this is therefore inescapable no matter how much of an activist one wants to be. I myself remember well that after I had passed my M.A. examination and was studying for my Ph.D. at Lahore, Mawdūdī remarked, after inquiring what I was studying, "The more you study, the more your practical faculties will be numbed. Why don't you come and join the Jamāʿat? The field is wide open." At that time my reply was, "Somehow, I love studying." And so it is no matter for surprise that, when a few years ago Mawdūdī decided to retire from the active leadership of the party, his successor was Miān Muḥammad Ṭufayl, an obviously well-meaning lawyer but without any pretensions whatever to Islamic scholarship.

Generally speaking, Pakistan has not been able to create an intellectual base for itself, a complicated phenomenon that needs special study. In the Islamic field one might expect her to have done better; yet it is here that her failure is not only most obvious but most disastrous as well, for an ideological state needs competent ideologues. Can the Jamāʿat-i-Islāmī produce any if the ulema cannot? This is also a question one might have justly asked I. H. Qureshī himself, whose strong words in condemnation of Pakistani intellectuals I quoted at the beginning of this section. He has justly called them cowardly. But on what basis could he explain his own wholesale espousal of the Jamʿiyat-i-Ṭalaba (the student wing of the Jamāʿat-i-Islāmī) throughout his tenure of the vice-chancellorship of the University of Karachi, which lasted more than a decade? There is no denying that Professor Qureshī was a serious intellectual, was a founding member of Pakistan, and was intellectually productive until his death. But the question I am asking is about his policies as head of the University of Karachi. His defense given in his just-quoted book (chap. 12), that it was the Jamʿiyat-i-Ṭalaba that could save young students from the radical left, hardly bears up under examination. For one thing, he exaggerates radical leftist presence at the early stages both in Pakistan and on university campuses. Leftism appeared all over Pakistan (particularly in the former East Pakistan) during the later years of the Ayūb Khān regime on the basis of the real or perceived economic polarization between the rich and the poor (this allegation had some real basis, although it was exaggerated out of proportion by the leftist propagandists, and I agree completely with Professor Qureshī that the middle classes, particularly the professionals, had in fact improved their standard of living beyond their expectations). But when leftism did appear in the form of Bhutto's People's party, did it not make short work of the moribund rightism of the Jamāʿat-i-Islāmī so much propagated in the name of Islam? Were the Jamʿiyat-i-Ṭalaba students then any match for the generally more alert and mentally agile leftists? Why did Professor Qureshī not institute a more enlightened and progressive curriculum in Islamic studies in the deparment of that name, which was created by him and where a book of essays culled from Mawdūdī's writings and edited by a teacher of economics (whose knowledge of Islam was essentially what Mawdūdī had given him) was made a textbook? It is true, and I shall presently say more on this, that the basic problem in Islamic studies has been teachers, but I have already pointed out that with the necessary goodwill and seriousness this vicious circle could have been successfully broken long ago. But one certainly cannot hope to stem the tide of historical forces, sweeping not only through Pakistan but through the whole of the Third World, with an army that is intellectually no more than paper tigers of Islam. This type of mentality has now been fully incarnated in the person of General Ziaul Haq, for whom election democracy is un-Islamic but a "monarchical form of government" is Islamically acceptable, a view held by no respectable Islamic thinker for almost a century.

I shall now briefly survey Islamic education in the public sector, that is, under official auspices since the creation of Pakistan. I have already noted that virtually no institution in the private sector has come up with either an improved curriculum or a new idea of a goal of Islamic education, or, indeed, better methods of teaching, unless the increase in the number of madrasas is itself considered an "improvement" in the field. At the time of partition, Pakistan had only one university, called the University of the Punjab, at Lahore. In the communal colleges attached to it, religious instruction was given as a "general subject," so that in the case of Islam, for example, no knowledge of Arabic was required. Attached to the university was the Oriental College, Lahore, where instruction in the languages and literatures of Islam and Hinduism was given and degrees were conferred. This college was a result of the desire of the British rulers to keep alive the study of the languages and cultures of Hindus and Muslims. Religions, as such, were therefore not taught, but cultures were; standards were relatively high.

After the creation of Pakistan, it was natural that enthusiasm for Islamic studies should sharply increase, which no doubt was the case. The university of the Punjab created an Islamiyāt Department in 1950; the next university to be established, that of Sind, founded a Department of Islamic History and Culture rather than Islamic studies (the reasons for this are not clear) in the early 1950s, those of Peshawar and Karachi followed in the late 1950s and early 1960s. The main problem, of course, as I pointed out earlier, was the unavailability of adequate teachers to man these departments—which is, indeed, the problem in this field all over the Muslim world. There were only three choices open—for the first two, one might either appoint relatively enlightened products of madrasas or appoint those modern scholars who had obtained Ph.D.s form Western universities and were already in higher institutions of learning as professors of Arabic, Persian, and Islamic history. It is curious that hardly any of them ever made Islam or Islamic studies the subject of doctoral research—one reason probably being that it would be odd for a Muslim to come to the West to learn Islam, and even if one did so one would not be accepted back home. Some people did study Sufism, but since the orthodox ulema have never regarded Sufism as a valid religious discipline—at any rate certainly not a central one—this was innocuous. Most people also undoubtedly feared that if they were to study Islam in the West and inevitably learned and applied critical and analytical methods to Islamic materials, they would be outcasts in their societies or even suffer persecution. Even the application of modern research methods to Islamic history, let alone to the Islamic materials themselves, had been generally very deficient. It is interesting that the severest critic of historic Islam in the subcontinent was a person who had had no modern training, Sayyid Aḥmad Khān. The next towering figure was Iqbāl, who was sharp and profound but was a philosopher by training and hardly knew any Arabic, and whose aim was not scholarship but reawakening of Muslims as a community. Still, most ulema disliked him intensely (just as they had disliked Aḥmad Khān) for his severe criticism of their lack of dynamism and forward-looking, even though Iqbāl himself was sometimes so solicitious of the ulema's opinion that he gave up a projected work on ijtihād on the advice of an ʿālim, Sayyid Sulaymān Nadvī.

Yet it is obvious that, if any progress was to be made toward the Islamic goals of the new state, the adoption of modern techniques of research was absolutely indispensable. The fear that applying these techniques would endanger Islam (just as they had damaged Christianity in the West) was ill-founded. The Qur'ān had been seen to be textually intact even by Western scholars, and the basic problem here was to evolve a valid method of interpreting the social content for modern needs. As for Ḥadīth, Aḥmad Khān and some of his colleagues had pronounced it unreliable long before Goldziher's work came out in the West. In fact, adoption of modern methods of research might well rehabilitate much Ḥadīth and even give it a proper place and meaning in historic Islam over against the extreme conclusions of Aḥmad Khān and his colleagues. In any case, no scholarly preparation had been made for the purposeful pursuit of Islamic studies in Pakistan, and the large bulk of modern Islamic scholars there as in other countries were more or less an adaptation of Western "orientalists." When I went to Oxford in 1946 for my doctoral work and met Sir S. Radhakrishnan, he asked me, "Why did you not go to Egypt rather than coming to Oxford?" "Islamic studies are pretty much as uncritical there as in India [those were prepartition days]," I replied. "That is a pity," replied Radhakrishnan, with an air as though the Hindu pundits had imbibed the spirit of modern critical research for Hindu materials! Besides, both in their nature and in their historical development, Islam and Hinduism were very different indeed.

If, therefore, there was a lack of adequate teachers for these departments in Pakistan, a fact Professor Qureshī rightly points out but wrongly bemoans (since he himself was a prominent intellectual in the Pakistan movement), whose fault was it? It was a failure of the community at large and particularly of the Muslim intellectual leadership and even more so of the "Muslim orientalists." Be that as it may, now more than three decades have elapsed in Pakistan, and what are the results today? Are there signs of a new intellectual development in this field? I am afraid Pakistani universities are only marking time. Professor Qureshī rightly says, again, that these developments cannot be expected to produce results overnight. The question is: Where are these developments in Pakistani unversities? No results can be expected even over the long run if a proper *beginning* is not made. I suspect that one vitiating factor in the universities (of which I know a certain amount by personal experience with some universities) is that standards for grading exams are deliberately lowered to "compete" with the rest of the universities (which take on a regional or provincial character).

The third of the three alternatives mentioned above was to appoint persons who had an emotional attachment to Islam and also a good deal of native intelligence but had neither a serious modern training nor yet a madrasa training—in general, of the order of Jamāʿat-i-Islāmī representatives or fellow-travelers. Now, in the absence of the second class discussed here at some length, universities had to appoint persons either from the first category—relatively enlightened madrasa products (as did Peshawar and Karachi)—or of the third type (as happened in Lahore). The University of Sind (at Hyderabad) appointed a scholar who had had a madrasa training and then earned an Oxford doctorate, and one would therefore expect much better results there. But such results were not forthcoming, and this illustrates brutally the real dimensions of the problem of intellectualism in Pakistan. Apart from the personal courage and steadfastness of an individual, the basic question is that of the general intellectual climate prevailing in the society. Pakistani society has not been able to evolve a solid, substantial intellectual climate. This is not the place to go into the reasons—a mad rush for a vast number of economically oriented jobs with their material attractions, as Professor Qureshī thinks, and, for some, innate fear of intellectual pursuits or the conviction that these are worthless, or indeed fear of social pressure—presumably all of these. The result is that the prepartition modernism has almost been wiped out; only its apologetic aspects have remained and thrived and acquired great vigor. If the name of Islam is still attached to the public sector, it is largely as a rallying point for the people through fear of (proved) Indian machinations, or the alternative may be what has now actually occurred, that a half-obscurantist fundamentalism has taken over in the form of a Jamāʿat-i-Islāmī type of "ideology."

During the regime of Muḥammad Ayūb Khān, however, three developments took place that are worthy of notice. In 1961 there was set up at Lahore under the auspices of the Department of Awqāf an ulema academy. This academy is doing useful though limited work by giving in-service training for a few weeks during which the already functioning ulema are also exposed to wider issues through lectures by administrators, economists, and such, and there are lengthy free panel discussions. It is clear, of course, that this activity, though obviously beneficial, is strictly limited in its scope.

In 1963, again under the aegis of the Awqāf Department, an institution of higher learning was set up by transforming an older madrasa titled Jāmiʿa ʿAbbāsiya (established by the Muslim ruler of Bahawalpur State in 1925), to which were attached several other smaller madrasas, into an Islamic university (al-Jāmiʿa al-Islāmiya). This institution has been visibly influenced in its curriculum by that of al-Azhar, and to the traditional subjects were added economics, history, geography, statistics, and philosophy. For the sake of government employment, its degree has been recognized as equivalent to that of a high school (of twelve years' training). The problem of teachers is of course acutely felt, but some khatībs I have met who graduated from this institution definitely represent an advance over graduates of the madrasas in that they are more aware that a new world exists outside the walls of the institution and that it presents many new problems—particularly social problems. It is too early, however, to make any firm predictions about the institution's future results (there are rumors that it is being now changed into a secular university under strong demands from the local population), but it is at present hardly a place that definitely promises to be a center of higher Islamic intellectualism.

The third institution, designed for higher Islamic research and interpretation and called "the Central Institute of Islamic Research" was also established by President Ayūb Khān in 1960; after the promulgation of the 1962 constitution, it was renamed "the Islamic Research Institute." Earlier, in 1954, the government had established an Institute of Islamic Culture at Lahore to popularize a modernist interpretation of Islam and to counteract extreme rightist and fundamentalist forces whose large-scale agitation for having the Aḥmadiya sect officially declared a non-Muslim minority had brought on a crisis in the spring of 1953 (the sect was eventually declared such by the National Assembly in September 1974). This institute, which is still functioning, did a good deal by way of publishing semipopular and popular works on Islam with a modernist point of view, but it did not, on the whole, address itself to the serious research and interpretation for which the Islamic Research Institute was created.[15] Obviously this institute faced the immediate problem of adequate human resources. During my tenure as director of the institute (1962–68) I tried a double strategy: to appoint some graduates of the madrasas with knowledge of English as junior fellows and try to give them training in modern research techniques and, conversely, to recruit junior fellows from among the university graduates in philosophy or social sciences and give them instruction in Arabic and in the essential classical Islamic disciplines like Ḥadīth and Islamic jurisprudence. I also sent several men abroad to get training and, where possible, degrees in Islamic studies in both Western and Eastern universities. My bid to invite a young post-doctoral Western scholar on a visiting appointment in order to work with and supervise the research work of the fellows—from the point of view not so much of content as of scientific research techniques and modern standards of sound scholarship—failed because no such scholar was available, even though I had braved strong resistance to this idea on the part of the influential daily the *Dawn* of Karachi. The institute was able to publish a periodical of serious scholarship, *Islamic Studies,* in which some good foreign scholars published their research materials and to which members of the institute also began to make contributions of acceptable quality, besides some books and critical editions of the classical texts.

15. Fazlur Rahman, "Some Religious Issues in the Ayub Khan Era," in *Essays on Islamic Civilization,* ed. Donald Little (Montreal: McGill University Press, 1974).

The case of this institute illustrates the real dilemma of purposeful and creative Islamic scholarship. On the one hand are the traditional madrasas, which are incapable of even conceiving what scientific scholarship is like and what its criteria are. On the other hand, there has been a constant flow of those scholars who have earned their Ph.D.s from Western universities—but in the process have become "orientalists." That is to say, they know enough of what sound scholarship is like, but their work is not Islamically purposeful or creative. They might write good enough works on Islamic history or literature, philosophy or art, but to think Islamically and to rethink Islam has not been one of their concerns. Obviously, in order to carry out Islamic purposes on the plane of thought, a purposeful, creative-interpretative study is a sine qua non, and this is precisely what is lacking. There is little doubt that this latter class of scholars wanted to avoid becoming controversial, and they much preferred a cozy corner in a university with a smug and secure career, but the question must be raised whether what they were doing was Islamic studies at all. In fact, several Western scholars have made important contributions to Islamic studies by producing new and genuine insights into the development of historic Islam, and, even though they are by definition, as it were, barred from contributing to normative Islam, many of their insights into historic Islam are important and relevant to a creative interpretation of normative Islam.

It is obvious that training scholars on these lines is fraught with difficulties. Even given the best will in the world, it is basically a question of whether or not the spark will ignite in a person's mind. Nor is the reinterpretation of Islam quite analogous to a reinterpretation of, say, Christianity, where the question is a theological interpretation of certain symbols. In Islam, on the other hand, reinterpretation primarily means a reworking and restructuring of sociomoral principles that will form the basis for a viable social Islamic fabric in the twentieth and twenty-first centuries. This will certainly imply an interpretation of the Muslim weltanschauung, picking up the threads from the Qur'ān itself and making the cosmic symbols relevant to the sociomoral principles—a task that has really not been achieved in medieval Islam, but that contemporary Islam requires much more than modern Christianity, for Islam, unlike Christianity, cannot be content with a mere theologicophilosophic vision.

But even as the institute was a little less than halfway through to the initial stage of its goal, it became the victim of a massive attack of the combined forces of the religious right and the opposition politicians. I resigned in September 1968 and the Ayūb Khān government fell six months later, and, although this group of progressive scholars has done its best to maintain itself, it has since been overwhelmed by the forces of reaction. Not only has the work of the institute deteriorated intellectually, there has been a constant pressure upon—indeed, threat to—its more enlightened members. This brings us back to the point noted earlier that the vitality of intellectual work depends bascially on a milieu of intellectual freedom; as I have remarked elsewhere, free thought and thought are synonymous, and one cannot hope that thought will survive without freedom. That Islamic thought must have certain purposes I have already insisted upon, but Islamic thought, like all thought, equally requires a freedom by which dissent, confrontation of views, and debate between ideas is assured. Finally, in 1980, the government created "Sharīʿa University" in Islamabad.

Some Remarks on Indonesia

It is notorious that in general accounts of Islam, let alone accounts of specific areas like Islamic law and education, Indonesia is severely ignored even though it is the most populous Muslim country, the general impression being that it is some sort of a "backwater" of Islam. Yet in more recent times there has been a high degree of Islamic intellectual activity in Indonesia. In the preceding chapter I noted the rise of the Muḥammadiya and the Nahḍat al-ʿUlamāʾ, the progressive and conservative wings of Indonesian Islam. But with independence a special and highly dynamic phase begins in Indonesia, not only in the political field, but in Islamic education as well. Although there is no comprehensive or even adequate work on the history of Islamic education in Indonesia in any Western language (the *Sedjarah Pendidikan Islam di Indonesia* is a good, informative book but is in Indonesian),[16] nevertheless certain basic developments can be discerned. (The Indonesian government has for some years now launched a program of scientific study of Islamic education

16. Mahmūd Junus [Yunus], *Sedjarah Pendidikan Islam di Indonesia* (Jakarta: Pustaka Mahmudiah, 1960).

in that country in which ministries of education and religious affairs are both involved, but so far little is known of this endeavor in the outside world.)

Like Pakistan and Turkey, and almost at the same time, Indonesia had to make a fresh start on Islamic education along modern lines. Turkey's genius for organization had produced a superb external structure for Islamic education; in Pakistan, as we saw in the preceding section, despite efforts, the development of Islamic intellectual life has been hampered by several factors, while in Indonesia, although Islam has experienced a great deal of difficulty in the political field, its educational efforts seem more fruitful. This last statement needs both substantiation and explanation, which is the task of this section. To begin with, Indonesia shares with all other major Muslim countries the basic problem of the modernization of Islamic education: the problem of lack of adequate personnel for teaching and research and of how to produce such personnel. There is therefore no escape from experimenting with a certain mélange of classical Islamic subjects with modern ones. These two are mixed in various proportions of the two ingredients depending on whether an institution belongs to the general educational system (where two compulsory sessions are devoted to Islamic instruction per week from the fourth through the twelfth grade and where from fifth grade on Arabic is taught as well), or to the progressive Muḥammadiya, where Islamic subjects might have an increasing preponderance over modern subjects as school years progress. There is also the arrangement, which appears to work quite well for some students, that a pupil attend a normal modern school during the day and get a madrasa education in the evening.

Through experimentation with various institutions called Islamic universities in Jakarta and Jogjakarta,[17] two institutes are now in existence (IAIN) for producing scholars of higher Islamic learning—one in Jakarta and the other in Jogjakarta. From their beginning in 1960, these IAINs (Institut Agama Islam Negeri—State Institute for Islam) have been duplicated in several other cities. The curriculum appears to have been patterned after al-Azhar's four faculties of theology, Sharīʿa, or Islamic law (al-Azhar, as I pointed out above, teaches secular and comparative law also in this faculty), education, or training of teachers, and

17. For details see B. J. Boland, *The Struggle of Islam in Modern Indonesia* (The Hague: Nijhoff, 1971).

adab, or Islamic humanities, with a particular emphasis on Arabic. Yet old madrasas and even pesantrins continue; the number of these in 1965 was estimated at about twenty-two thousand. Many higher Islamic institutions in Indonesia, like those in Turkey, but unlike those in Pakistan, rightly stress the learning of Arabic, and many Indonesian students and scholars, like those in Turkey, can speak *classical* Arabic fluently. Many Indonesian institutions maintain contacts with al-Azhar by means of visiting professors from that university, as well as large numbers of Indonesian students sent to study at al-Azhar. Now that the government of Indonesia has started a major research effort on Islamic education, it is quite likely that most madrasas and pesantrins will become feeder institutions to the state institutes for Islam.

But far more important than the extensiveness of Islamic education (and it does appear to be very extensive, for the number of students at the Islamic institutions—although no accurate statistics are available—is said to be several million) and its external structure is the question of the intellectual quality of the products of this system of education. Since the state institutes for Islam, like comparable institutions in almost all other major Muslim countries, are quite recent, it is impossible to make any predictions. The soil of Indonesia, Java in particular, with its wild growth of all sorts of organized spiritualities—most of which are either survivals from or recrudescences of pre-Islamic religions—could on principle furnish an excellent climate for the growth of a progressive interpretation of Islam, and there is no doubt that on certain important social, economic, and political issues that are proving to be poisonous hang-ups in the Middle Eastern Islamic societies (questions of segregation of women, bank interest, and Islamic socioeconomic justice or "Islamic socialism"), Indonesian Islam has cast its die for progress. But a miscalculation of the religious situation in Indonesia, where these wilder anomian, or even antinomian, spiritualities have from time to time tantalized rulers as forms of religious liberalism and escapes from conservative or fundamentalist Islam, could backfire with disastrous results—despite the statements of many Western scholarly observers and analysts. There appears to be a widespread belief in these circles and even in many Indonesian groups that if only these "spiritual" ideologies could succeed, then their quiescent waters, rid of stormy conservative and fundamentalist activism, could be channeled in any "liberal" direction. The basic trouble with this view is that in the depths of such "spiritual" waters, there are hardly ever to be found any "social pearls." And without denying the value and, indeed, necessity of the spiritual element in the life of the individuals, it also seems indisputable that no spiritualism per se has been positively conducive to the establishment of *any* moral-social order, which is the desideratum of all world societies today. Islam can yield such an order if suitably interpreted, for that was its very original impulse. The problem of ridding Muslims of a certain "hard crust" of tradition is a formidable one and has to be faced, but the way out is certainly not to confront it with vagrant amorphous spiritualities. Indeed, the more Islam is confronted with these or other superficial forms of liberalism, the more likely it is to recoil upon itself and the more hardened its traditional crust may become. Nor is it within the power of any government to disregard Islam: the only way to secure tolerance for non-Islamic religions is to get it from within Islam, and no liberalism that used illiberal means to establish itself ever succeeded. The Indonesian people are themselves a democratic people by temperament, and only a genuinely democratic interpretation of Islam can succeed there.

Indeed, judging from the history of Islamic publications in recent years, the situation can hardly be called discouraging. The voluminous commentary on the Qur'ān in Indonesian by Hasbi Ash-Shiddiqy (al-Siddīqī) is said to contain systematic accounts of the background of the Qur'ānic verses (the "occasions of revelation"), a development that is a desideratum in many Muslim countries and without which it is impossible to understand the purposes of the Qur'ān in the social and legal spheres. This approach to an understanding of the Qur'ān should naturally end up in a wider sociohistorical approach, which is the only adequate method to understand the social values (rather than legal enactments) of the Qur'ān. Indonesian translations of al-Ghazālī and Ibn Khaldūn have been made available and are read. Apparently the original gap between the traditionalists (the Nahḍat al-ʿUlamā') and the reformists (the Muḥammadiya) has been almost closed, and I myself have heard certain prominent members of the former discussing not just the theoretical possibility, but actual ijtihād solutions to certain social problems. I regard it as likely that, given time, opportunity, and facilities,

Indonesian Islam, although currently and understandably heavily dependent on al-Azhar, will develop a meaningful indigenous Islamic tradition that will be genuinely Islamic and creative. Although the present state of affairs obviously needs much improvement, there are signs of hope for the future: the feverish educational and intellectual activity, although recent, appears to be heading in the right direction.

4

Prospects and Some Suggestions

Statement of the Problem

Muḥammad Shiblī Nuʿmānī wrote in his *Safarnāma* (his own account of his visit to the Middle East, May–October 1892), after talking about the potential benefits of the Dār al-ʿUlūm at Cairo, "But those people who have been once as much as touched by traditional education, remain forever irreconcilably estranged from modern learning."[1] In the same work he quotes Muḥammad ʿAbduh as saying to him, after bemoaning the plight of al-Azhar, about the Egyptian products of Western education. "These are even more misguided."[2] This dilemma that characterized education in the days of Shiblī and ʿAbduh in the "forward" lands of Islam—lands that had a highly developed traditional education as well as a recently adopted modern Western-style education—is, as the preceding pages have demonstrated, still as real today. The reason is that, despite a widespread and sometimes deep consciousness of the dichotomy of education, all efforts at a genuine integration have so far been largely unfruitful.

Let us first analyze more closely the basic features of the attempts at reforming education insofar as Islam is concerned. There are basically two aspects of this reformist orientation. One approach is to accept modern secular education as it has developed generally speaking in the West and to attempt to "Islamize"

1. Muḥammad Shiblī Nuʿmānī, *Safarnāma* (Lahore: Ghulam ʿAli and Sons, 1961), pp. 285–86.
2. Ibid., p. 349.

it—that is, to inform it with certain key concepts of Islam. This approach has had two distinct goals, although they are not always distinguished from one another: first, to mold the *character* of students with Islamic values for individual and collective life, and, second, to enable the adepts of modern education to imbue their respective fields of learning at higher levels, using an Islamic perspective to transform, where necessary, both the content and the orientation of these fields. The two goals are closely connected in the sense that molding character with Islamic values is naturally undertaken bsically at the primary level of education when students are young and impressionable. However, if nothing is done to imbue fields of higher learning with an Islamic orientation, or if attempts to do so are unsuccessful, when young boys and girls reach the higher stages of education their outlook is bound to be secularized, or they are very likely to shed whatever Islamic orientation they have had—which has been happening on a large scale.

"Imbuing higher fields of learning with Islamic values" is a phrase whose meaning must be made more precise. All human knowledge may be divided into what are called "natural" or exact sciences, whose generalizations are called "laws of nature," and the fields of learning that have been called "humanities" and "social sciences." Although the *content* of physical or exact sciences cannot by definition be interfered with—else they will be falsified—their orientation can be given a value character. Sometimes certain mistaken ideological attitudes try to interfere with the content of these sciences as well, as, for example, when Stalin ordered Russian biologists to emphasize the influence of environment at the expense of heredity. Under such influences or pressures, science must become a mockery, but it is possible and highly desirable for a scientist to know the consequences his investigations have for mankind. It is also equally and, indeed, urgently important for scientific knowledge to be a unity and to give an overall picture of the universe in order to answer the all-important questions, "Does it mean anything? Does it point to a higher will and purpose? Or is it, to use Whitehead's famous words, "a mere hurrying of material endlessly, meaninglessly"? The first is a practical question, the second a "theoretical" one but with obvious practical implications.

Social sciences and humanities are obviously relevant to values, and values are relevant to them. This is of course not to say that they are subjective, although subjectivism often does enter into them, sometimes palpably. But to be value oriented is certainly not by itself to be subjective, provided values do not remain mere assumptions but are "objectified." Although metaphysical speculation is the area of human intellectual endeavor that is perhaps the remotest from factual objectivity, yet it need not be, as Bradley put it, "the finding of bad reasons for what we already believe on instinct." If metaphysics enjoys the least freedom from assumed premises, man enjoys the least freedom from metaphysics in that metaphysical beliefs are the most ultimate and pervasively relevant to human attitudes; it is consciously or unconsciously the source of all values and of the meaning we attach to life itself. It is therefore all-important that this very ground of formation of our attitudes be as much informed as possible. Positivism may be negative enough to dismiss it as "meaningless"; yet positivism had rendered great service to a genuine metaphysics by exploding the empty thought shell in which the greatest human minds used to incarcerate themselves. Metaphysics, in my understanding, is the unity of knowledge and the meaning and orientation this unity gives to life. If this unity is the unity of knowledge, how can it be all that subjective? It is a faith grounded in knowledge.

There has not been much by way of an Islamic metaphysics, at least in modern times. In the medieval centuries there were Muslim metaphysicians, some of them brilliant, original, and influential; but the primary basis of their entire weltanschauung was Hellenic thought, not the Qurʾān. Some of their doctrines were repugnant to the orthodoxy, which took such fright that down the centuries all metaphysical thought became anathema to it. Among the orthodox there has not been a lack of men of deep insight, but there has been no systematic and coherent body of metaphysical thought fully informed by the Qurʾānic weltanschauung, which is itself remarkably coherent. In modern times, Muḥammad Iqbāl's *Reconstruction of Religious Thought in Islam* is the only systematic attempt. But, despite the fact that Iqbāl had certain basic and rare insights into the nature of Islam as an attitude to life, this work cannot be said to be based on Qurʾānic teaching: the structural elements of its thought are too contemporary to be an adequate basis for an ongoing Islamic metaphysical endeavor (although I certainly disagree with H. A. R. Gibb's asessment according to which Ashʿarite theology, for example, is more faithful to the Qurʾānic matrix of ideas than Iqbāl's thought). What is true is that Iqbāl's thought, like all modern liberal thought, is essentially a *personal* effort, while Ashʿarī's theology, as a credal system, consisted of certain formal principles that he claimed to have drawn from the Qurʾān and on the basis of which he elaborated a full-fledged theological system. But, besides the question whether a modern outlook can have room for hard-and-fast and cut-and-dried formal creeds, this does not mean that Ashʿarite theology represented Islam more faithfully than did Iqbāl; on the contrary, that theology represents, in my view, an almost total distortion of Islam and was, in fact, a one-sided and extreme reaction to the Muʿtazilite rationalist theology.

However, to resume what I was saying about the Muslims' aim of Islamizing the several fields of learning, this aim cannot be really fulfilled unless Muslims effectively perform the intellectual task of elaborating an Islamic metaphysics on the basis of the Qurʾān. An overall world view of Islam has to be first, if provisionally, attempted if various specific fields of intellectual endeavor are to cohere as informed by Islam. In medieval Islam, even if Ashʿarite theology was Islamically wayward, it certainly tried—sometimes with remarkable efficiency—to permeate the intellectual disciplines of Islam, like law, Sufism, and even the outlook on history. In modern times, however, although many Muslims are conscious of the desirability and even necessity of investing factual knowlege with Islamic values, the result is so far perhaps less than negligible—although there is no dearth of booklets and pamphlets on "Islam and this" and "Islam and that," which occasionally do contain valuable insights and often a good deal of ingenuity but are essentially marred by an apologetic attitude. More recently, a number of conferences and seminars have been held in Saudi Arabia and Pakistan (the former's latter-day spiritual client) on such topics as "Islam and Education," "Islam and Economics," or "Islam and Psychology." I have not seen any publications so far, if any have resulted from this feverish activity. One cannot, of course, expect any spectacular results as yet, but the effort is worth continuing.

I said earlier that the effort to inculcate an Islamic character in young students is not likely to succeed if the higher fields of learning remain completely secular, that is, unpurposeful with regard to their effect on the future of mankind. Indeed, even in the West, attempts at molding young students' character have failed because when these boys and girls grow up they find all life around them practically secular, and they become disillusioned with their childhood orientation, which comes to seem a kind of "pious fraud." In fact, they often grow up with a vengeance and, barring other factors to the contrary, become more secular-minded than their parents. The same is very much true of Muslim children, although in Muslim society the social temper still plays a major role in curbing open deviations and utter secularization. But if moral values are thus observed or at least not flouted under social pressure, this hardly goes altogether to the credit of the efficacy of the Islamic spirit. We shall have to come back later to this all-important issue; in the meantime, we must discuss the problem of what is meant by reforming Islamic education itself since, unless some solution to this is forthcoming, it is futile even to raise the question of the Islamization of knowledge: it is the upholders of Islamic learning who have to bear the primary responsibility of Islamizing secular knowledge by their creative intellectual efforts.

In essence, then, the whole problem of "modernizing" Islamic education, that is, rendering it capable of creative Islamic intellectual productivity in all fields of intellectual endeavor together with the serious commitment to Islam that the madrasa system has generally been able to impart, is the problem of expanding the Muslim's intellectual vision by raising his intellectual standards. For expansion of vision is a function of rising to heights; the lower down you come the less space you can see, and the more you think yourself master of that little space under your narrow vision. And here appears the stark contrast between the actual Muslim attitudes and the demands of the Qur'ān. The Qur'ān sets a very high value on knowledge, and the Prophet himself is ordered to pray to God: "O Lord! increase my knowledge" (20:114). Indeed, the Qur'ān itself is firmly of the view that the more knowledge one has the more capable of faith and commitment one will be. There is absolutely no other view of the relationship of faith and knowledge that one can legitimately derive from the Qur'ān. It is true that the Qur'ān is highly critical, for example, of Meccan tradesmen who "know well the externalities of the lower [i.e., material] life but are heedless of its ends" (30:7). But this is precisely the point I am making here—that a knowledge that does not expand the horizons of one's vision and action is truncated and injurious knowledge. But how can one have knowledge of the "ends" of life—that is, of higher values—without knowing actual reality? If the Muslim modernist has done nothing else, he has adduced such formidable evidence from the Qur'ān for the absolute necessity to faith of a knowledge of the universe, of man, and of history, that all Muslims today at least pay lip service to it.

But, by contrast, the Muslim attitude to knowledge in the later medieval centuries is so negative that if one puts it beside the Qur'ān one cannot help being appalled. According to this attitude, higher knowledge and faith are mutually dysfunctional and increase at each other's expense. Knowledge thus appears to be purely secular, as is basically the case with all "modern" positive knowledge—indeed, even modern "religious" knowledge is secular, or else it is considered positively injurious to faith. Sometimes an arbitrary distinction is drawn between "religious" and "nonreligious" sciences; the former have, of course, to be acquired at the expense of the latter. Sometimes a distinction is drawn between the "more urgent" knowledge—that of law and/or theological propositions—and "the less urgent or less important" positive sciences. And often enough, indeed, a distinction is drawn between "good" knowledge and "bad" knowledge, for example, of philosophy or music, while a third category is posited of more or less "useless" knowledge such as mathematics. There are several causes of these pernicious distinctions. One of these I have already pointed out, namely, the fear of philosophy and of intellectualism in general. Another important reason certainly was, as I indicated in chapter 2, that a knowledge of orthodox disciplines, particularly of law, was an almost sure passport to employment, whereas mathematics or astronomy brought little by way of a livelihood, let alone of fame, and medicine was accepted as a necessary though inferior endeavor. Al-Ghazālī, in his criticism of a slogan of medical men, "First [attend to] your body and then [to] your religion [or soul]"—"*badanak thumma dīnak,*" typifies the medieval orthodox attitude to medicine when he says that by such catchy slogans these people want to deceive the simpleminded public as to the real order of priorities.

Whatever the reason, the stark contrast between the Qur'ān and the medieval Muslim pursuits of knowledge is obvious. During approximately the past one hundred years, as the preceding two chapters show, Muslims have displayed an increasing awareness of reforming traditional education and integrating the old knowledge with the modern. But this development has been marred by certain important, indeed, fundamental weaknesses that it is essential to elucidate before we can look at the future with greater clarity and a more constructive outlook. The first important block to any reform is the phenomenon I have called neorevivalism or neofundamentalism. Before the advent of classical modernism, there had existed a revivalism or fundamentalism since the eighteenth century. The "Wahhābī" movement and other kindred or parallel reform phenomena wanted to reconstruct Islamic spirituality and morality on the basis of a return to the pristine "purity" of Islam. The current postmodernist fundamentalism, in an important way, is novel because its basic élan is anti-Western (and, by implication of course, anti-Westernism). Hence its condemnation of classical modernism as a purely Westernizing force. Classical modernists were, of course, not all of a piece, and it is true that some of these modernists went to extremes in their espousal of Western thought, morality, society, and so on. Such phenomena are neither unexpected nor unnatural when rapid change occurs, particularly when it derives from a living source like the West. But just as the classical modernist had picked upon certain specific issues to be considered and modernist positions to be adopted thereupon—democracy, science, status of women, and such—so now the neofundamentalist, after—as I said before—borrowing certain things from classical modernism, largely rejected its content and, in turn, picked upon certain specific issues as "Islamic" par excellence and accused the classical modernist of having succumbed to the West and having sold Islam cheaply there. The pet issues with the neofundamentalist are the ban on bank interest, the ban on family planning, the status of women (contra the modernist), collection of zakāt, and so forth—things that will most *distinguish* Muslims from the West. Thus, while the modernist was engaged by the West through attraction, the neorevivalist is equally haunted by the West through repulsion. The most important and urgent thing to do from this point of view is to "disengage" mentally from the West and to cultivate an independent but understanding attitude toward it, as toward any other civilization, though more particularly to the West because it is the source of much of the social change occurring throughout the world.

So long as Muslims remain mentally locked with the West in one way or the other, they will not be able to act independently and autonomously.

The neorevivalist has undoubtedly served as a corrective not only for several types of excesses in classical modernism but, above all, for secularist trends that would otherwise have spread much faster in Muslim societies. That is to say, neorevivalism has reoriented the modern-educated lay Muslim *emotionally* toward Islam. But the greatest weakness of neorevivalism, and the greatest disservice it has done to Islam, is an almost total lack of positive effective Islamic thinking and scholarship within its ranks, its intellectual bankruptcy, and its substitution of cliché mongering for serious intellectual endeavor. It has often contended, with a real point, that the learning of the conservative traditional ulema, instead of turning Muslims toward the Qurʾān, has turned them away from it. But its own way of turning to the Qurʾān has been no more than, as I said above, picking upon certain selected issues whereby it could crown itself by "distinguishing" Muslims from the rest of the world, particularly from the West. The traditionalist ulema, if their education has suffered from a disorientation toward the purposes of the Qurʾān, have nevertheless built up an imposing edifice of learning that invests their personalities with a certain depth; the neorevivalist is, by contrast, a shallow and superficial person—really rooted neither in the Qurʾān nor in traditional intellectual culture, of which he knows practically nothing. Because he has no serious intellectual depth or breadth, his consolation and pride both are to chant ceaselessly the song that Islam is "very simple" and "straightforward," without knowing what these words mean. In a sense, of course, the Qurʾān is simple and uncomplicated, as is all genuine religion—in contradistinction to theology—but in another and more meaningful sense a book like the Qurʾān, which gradually appeared over almost twenty-three years, is highly complicated—as complicated as life itself. The essence of the matter is that the neorevivalist has produced *no* Islamic educational system worthy of the name, and this is primarily because, having become rightly dissatisfied with much of the traditional learning of the ulema, he himself has been unable to devise any methodology, any structural strategy, for understanding Islam or for interpreting the Qurʾān.

Second, the reform efforts that have taken place so far have been in two directions. In one direction, this reform has occurred almost entirely within the framework of traditional education itself. Generated largely by the premodernist reform phenomena whose impetus still continues to some extent, this reform has tended to "simplify" the traditional syllabus, which it finds heavily loaded with "extraneous" materials such as medieval theology, certain branches of philosophy (such as logic), and a plethora of works on Islamic law. This simplification consists in dropping most or all works in these medieval disciplines and accentuating Ḥadīth, occasionally Arabic language and literature, and, in certain cases, principles of Qur'ānic interpretation (but not the Qur'ān—i.e., its text—as such), in consistency with the religious ideology of these premodernist reformist movements that aimed to "purify" Islam from later accretions. This is confirmed by the developments concerning the subcontinent that I sketched out toward the end of chapter 1.

In the second direction, a variety of developments have occurred that can be summed up by saying that they all represent an effort to combine and integrate the modern branches of learning with the old ones. In such cases, the years of curriculum have been extended and brought in line with the curricular span of modern schools and colleges, or, as I noted for Indonesia, supplemented by afternoon classes held after the modern lay education of the present-day schools—thus lengthening the day rather than increasing the number of curricular years. At the college level, however, even in the Indonesian experiment, the effort is directed at combining modern subjects with the old.

The most important of these experiments are undoubtedly those of al-Azhar of Egypt and the new system of Islamic education introduced in Turkey since the late 1940s. Al-Azhar has behind it a long tradition of medieval Islamic learning, and therefore, understandably, its conservatism in the field of religious studies is still very strong. Consequently, the modern subjects like philosophy, sociology, and psychology do not seem to have a deep impact, since they essentially trail behind the medieval learning. In Turkey, on the other hand, where traditional education had been completely destroyed, it is being reintroduced afresh, while the modern disciplines are almost at the same level as in the lay schools—indeed, all over in the developing countries. Turkey is fortunate in having to make a fresh start because it has the opportunity to interpret the medieval intellectual heritage and give it a new shape—which, as we shall see presently, is a basic desideratum in all current attempts to integrate the modern and the traditional and which has been satisfied only to a limited degree at al-Azhar in the fields of theology and law.

At present, the "integration" I spoke of above is basically absent because of the largely mechanical character of instruction and because of juxtaposition of the old with the new. It is true that all these reforms are confronted with a vicious circle in that, on the one hand, unless adequate teachers are available with minds already integrated and creative, instruction will remain sterile even given goodwill and talent on the part of students, while, on the other, such teachers cannot be produced on a sufficient scale unless, substantively speaking, an integrated curriculum is made available. This vicious circle can be broken only at the first point—if there come into being some first-class minds who can interpret the old in terms of the new as regards substance and turn the new into the service of the old as regards ideals. This, then, must be followed by the writing of new textbooks on theology, ethics, and so forth. Such minds cannot be produced at will, but something can certainly be done in this respect—namely to recruit from the best talent available and to provide the necessary incentives for a committed intellectual career in this field. Today, most of the students who are attracted to this field are those who have failed to gain entrance to more lucrative careers. This shows how little awareness there is that creating minds is both more difficult and, in the last analysis, more urgent than constructing bridges. There is little doubt that most Eastern societies have been laboring under the false and totally self-deceptive impression that they suffer from an overplentitude of spirituality and spiritual insights while the West, barren in this respect, has outstripped them in material technology and that now they need only get the latter. That the West has outstripped the East in science and technology is correct; what seems to be a fiction is that the East is replete with spirituality, for, if this were so, why should the East—or the Muslim societies—suffer from the mental and spiritual dichotomy of which I have mainly been speaking here?

Second, an important problem that has plagued Muslim societies since the dawn of democracy in them is the peculiar relationship of religion and politics and the pitiable subjugation of the former to the latter. Indeed, it was this pernicious phenomenon that forced Kemāl Atatürk to opt for secularism. Secularism is not the answer—quite the opposite. But the politics being waged most of the time in these countries is hardly less pernicious in its effects than secularism itself. For, instead of setting themselves to genuinely interpret Islamic goals to be realized through political and government channels—which would subjugate politics to interpreted Islamic values (whether these values or goals turn out to be conservative or liberal, fundamentalist or modern for different parties)—what happens most of the time is a ruthless exploitation of Islam for party politics and group interests that subjects Islam not only to politics but to day-to-day politics; Islam thus becomes sheer demagoguery. Unfortunately, the so-called Islamic parties in several countries are the most blatantly guilty of such systematic political manipulation of religion. The slogan "in Islam religion and politics are inseparable" is employed to dupe the common man into acceptng that, instead of politics or the state serving the long-range objectives of Islam, Islam should come to serve the immediate and myopic objectives of party politics. Reform and reconstruction of that powerful instrument for the shaping of minds—education—is inconceivable in these circumstances. The secularist, who is in any case already alienated from Islam, becomes all the more confirmed in his cynicism about men of religion, the dislocation between their aims and their claims, even though secularism itself may be a child of incurable cynicism about man's real nature.

And yet the most important single channel of both these latter reforms—the correct envisioning of priorities and the saving of religion from the vagaries of day-to-day politics—is education itself. I must therefore turn to a consideration of the possible solution to the problems I have raised in the field of the reform of Islamic education itself: how it can become meaningful in the modern intellectual and spiritual setting, not so much to save religion from modernity—which is, after all, only a partisan interest—but to save modern man from himself through religion.

Some Considerations toward a Solution

Toward an Understanding of Islam

The first essential step to relieve the vicious circle just mentioned is, for the Muslim, to distinguish clearly between normative Islam and historical Islam. Unless effective and sustained efforts are made in this direction, there is no way visible for the creation of the kind of Islamic mind I have been speaking of just now. No amount of mechanical juxtaposition of old and new subjects and disciplines can produce this kind of mind. If the spark for the modernization of old Islamic learning and for the Islamization of the new is to arise, then the original thrust of Islam—of the Qurʾān and Muḥammad—must be clearly resurrected so that the conformities and deformities of historical Islam may be clearly judged by it. In the first chapter I indicated by what process this normative Islam had understandably, perhaps inevitably, but often by no means justifiably passed into its historical forms. In that chapter I also indicated how this resurrection may be accomplished—namely, by studying the Qurʾān's social pronouncements and legal enactments in the light of its general moral teaching and particularly under the impact of its stated objectives (or principles, if one prefers this expression) on the one hand and against the background of their historical-social milieu on the other. Since this method has been made fairly clear in that chapter and particularly in the Introduction, there is no need to repeat it here, but certain other questions concerning it must be answered.

Is this method not yet another form of fundamentalism that will once again, in a new and more "scientific" way, create another idol to arrest Muslims' forward progress? After all, all fundamentalists, like the Wahhābīs and subsequently their neofundamentalist successors such as the Ikhwān, have just said this, namely, that Muslims must go back to the original and pristine Islam; yet they have been arrested at a certain point. Again, the Muslim modernist has also explicitly held that Muslims must go back to the original and pristine Islam; yet they have come up with certain doctrines that both the fundamentalist and the conservative have failed to recognize as Islamic—indeed, as anything but Western, that is, un-Islamic! What is, then the guarantee, or at least the likelihood, that the pursuit of the new solution will not be arrested at a certain point, or that the results reached will not be so bewilderingly chaotic and contradictory?

The answer is that neither the fundamentalist nor the modernist had a clear enough method. That fundamentalist movements in Islam have been arrested is not due to their claims, for they claimed ijtihād, that is, new thinking in Islam. How can anyone arrest new thought, particularly when it is claimed that the essence of the Islamic thought process rests on ijtihād? Actually it is even something of a misnomer to call such phenomena in Islam "fundamentalist" except insofar as they emphasize the basis of Islam as being the two original sources: the Qurʾān and the Sunna of the Prophet Muḥammad. Otherwise they emphasize ijtihād, original thought, which is something forbidden by Western fundamentalists who, while emphasizing the Bible as the "fundament," reject original or new thought. It is also something of an irony to pit the so-called Muslim fundamentalists against the Muslim modernists, since, so far as their acclaimed procedure goes, the Muslim modernists say exactly the same thing as the so-called Muslim fundamentalists say: that Muslims must go back to the original and definitive sources of Islam and perform ijtihād on that basis.

To resume my answer to this important question: the so-called fundamentalists and modernists have come up with radically different answers to some basic issues acording to their respective environments, but neither has had a clear enough method of interpreting the Qurʾān and the Sunna. As I pointed out in the previous section, the neorevivalist has no method worthy of the name except to react, on certain important social issues, to the classical modernist. I also pointed out earlier that the classical modernist had no method except to treat ad hoc issues that seemed to him to require solution for Muslim society but that were historically of Western inspiration and that he attempted to solve, often with remarkable plausibility, in the light of Qurʾānic teaching. As for the premodernist revivalist, he had certainly worked within the traditional perimeters of Islam and had found that Muslim individual and collective life had become permeated with degrading superstitions that, according to the Qurʾānic monotheism, were a form of *shirk* and must therefore be eradicated. This was undoubtedly sound, but for the rest the premodernist revivalist neither had nor bothered to seek a methodology of Qurʾānic interpretation that would be sound in scholarship, rationally reliable, and faithful to the Qurʾān itself.

Although the method I have advocated here is new in form, nevertheless its elements are all traditional. It is the biographers of the Prophet, the Ḥadīth collectors, the historians, and the Qurʾān commentators who have preserved for us the general social-historical background of the Qurʾān and the Prophet's activity and in particular the background (*sha'n al-nuzūl*) of the particular passages of the Qurʾān—despite the divergence of accounts about the latter in some cases. This would surely not have been done but for their strong belief that this background is necessary for our understanding of the Qurʾān. It is strange, however, that no systematic attempt has ever been made to understand the Qurʾān in the order in which it was revealed, that is, by setting the specific cases of the *shu'un al-nuzūl,* or "occasions of revelation," in some order in the general background that is no other than the activity of the Prophet (the Sunna in the proper sense) and its social environment. If this method is pursued, most arbitrary and fanciful interpretations will at once be ruled out, since a definite enough anchoring point will be available. It is only because the Qurʾān was not treated as a coherent whole by many Muslim thinkers that the metaphysical part, which should form the necessary backdrop to a coherent elaboration of the moral, social, and legal message of the Qurʾān, in particular received the wildest interpretations at the hands of the so-called esoteric school, be they Sufis, Bāṭinīs, philosophers, or even some *mutakallimūn* (theologians), while the majority of the orthodox became dusty-dry literalists far removed from any genuine insight into the depths of the Qurʾān. The Qurʾān, despite its distinction within its own body of "firm" and "ambiguous" verses (3:7)—which has been made so much of by several speculative minds, but which seems to refer to verses of specific and general import—categorically states in numerous places that it is coherent and that it is free from inconsistencies—a claim that is well attested by any closer study of it, which is not vitiated by extravagant preconceived notions (e.g., 11:1, 22:52, 4:82, and all such verses where the Qurʾān speaks of itself as *tafṣīl,* i.e., a "firm exposition"). Indeed, verse 3:7 itself strongly suggests—and it has very often been so interpreted—that the "ambiguous" verses are to be taken in the light of, although in turn as being matricial to, the "firm" ones.

Yet none of this means that any significant interpretation of the Qurʾān can be absolutely monolithic. Nothing could be further from the truth. For one thing, we know from numerous reports that the Prophet's Companions themselves sometimes understood certain Qurʾānic verses differently, and this was within his knowledge. Further, the Qurʾān, as I have often reiterated, is a document that grew within a background, from the flesh and blood of actual history; it is therefore both as "straightforward" and as organically coherent as life itself. Any attempt to take it with a literalist, partialist superficiality and lifeless rigidity will, to use A. J. Arberry's phrase, "crush its gossamer wings to powder." For example, on the question of murder, the Qurʾān essentially confirms the pre-Islamic Arab forms of settlement either by blood money or by "life for life," adding that forgiveness is better. From this, all our lawyers deduced the principle that murder is a private crime against the bereaved family, which has therefore to decide whether the murderer will be forgiven, whether he should pay for the murder in money, or whether he should be killed in revenge. However, the Qurʾān also enunciates a more general principle stating that "whosoever kills a person unrightfully or without a mischief [i.e., a war] on the earth, it is as though he has killed all humanity; while he who saves one person, it is as though he has saved all humanity" (5:32), which obviously makes murder a crime against society rather than a private crime against a family. But our lawyers never brought this verse to bear on the issue of murder.

To insist on absolute uniformity of interpretation is therefore neither possible nor desirable. What is important is first of all to use the kind of method I am advocating to eliminate vagrant interpretations. For the rest, every interpreter must explicitly state his general assumptions with regard to Qurʾānic interpretation in general and specific assumptions and premises with regard to specific issues or passages. Once his assumptions are made explicit, then discussion among differing interpreters is possible and subjectivity is further reduced. But the kinds of differences about the conception of God—whether he is the ground of the being that manifests itself through every existent and is therefore to be contemplated, or whether he is the ultimate and transcendent principle that has simply to be established and "proved" like a mathematical formula, or whether he is the creator-commander who has to be worshiped and obeyed, and so forth—should surely be capable of being sorted out for public and collective life at least, leaving scope for private idiosyncrasies, which in any case cannot cease.

Such interpretive attempts can be made by individual scholars, but they can obviously be made by teamwork as well. What is certain is that there have to be several attempts so that, through discussion and debate, the community at large can accept some interpretations and discard others. It is obviously not necessary that a certain interpretation once accepted must continue to be accepted; there is always both room and necessity for new interpretations, for this is, in truth, an ongoing process. But such bona fide attempts by competent scholars are, as I said before, the only way to break the vicious circle of "where to start" the process of reform in Islamic education. For the first logical step now is the creation of new intellectual materials, since the mechanical part of the process of reform in terms of combining old and new subjects in new reformed schools or setting up afternoon Islamic schools to supplement the morning "regular schools" is by now well underway in virtually all Muslim lands.

Nor is this first step impossible to achieve. The greatest difficulty that will be experienced is not the new step itself but extricating one's feet from the stagnant waters of the old Qur'ānic exegesis, which may contain many pearls but which, on the whole, impedes rather than promotes a real understanding of the Qur'ān. Qur'ān commentaries are, of course, not all of the same value, some being purely subjective distortions, others of real importance in providing both insight and historical information; but the approach being advocated herein is new—although, as I said before, its elements are all in the tradition itself. The new step simply consists in studying the Qur'ān in its total and specific background (and doing this study systematically in a historical order), not just studying it verse by verse or passage by passage with an isolated "occasion of revelation" (sha'n al-nuzūl).

Reconstruction of the Islamic Sciences

The Historical Period

The proposition that the Sharīʿa law and institutions have to be derived methodically and systematically from the Qur'ān and the example of the Prophet (i.e., his total performance) in the manner described above does not mean that Islamic sciences, as they have originated and developed historically, have to be ignored or discarded. Indeed, they *cannot* be ignored or discarded for certain basic reasons. First of all, it is historic Islam that gives continuity to the intellectual and spiritual being of the community. No community can annul its past and hope to create a future being for itself—as that community. A basic fallacy of an Atatürkish kind of "reform" consists precisely in an effort to shed the historical being of the community and to seek a future without it. It is important, however, to understand precisely the meaning of what I am saying, which is *not* that we should necessarily go slow with reform through gradual steps by a process of partial and ad hoc adjustments. My argument has been, in fact, *against* an ad hoc policy, because, whatever its practical wisdom (which is dubious), it necessarily distorts vision by making it myopic. And it is, in any case, a policy Muslims can ill afford at the present juncture, since the gap between what is and what ought to be is much too great. It must also constantly be borne in mind that the Muslim community has developed over the centuries (say, since the tenth/eleventh) a temper whereby it can swallow small changes without perceptibly moving forward. The factor that has produced this tremendous digestive power can be called conservatism or the spirit of ijmāʿ (consensus), depending upon the point of view one chooses to adopt, but the fact remains that it is extremely difficult to move the community as a whole. If one studies the vast and rich juristic and speculative literature of Islam (even leaving out the protean Sufism), one finds startling, indeed, revolutionary ideas in the writings of men who were high "orthodox" authorities, but none of these have left any trace on the being of the community. Changes in the community have always occurred when the cumulative process has reached a stage of outburst that literally re-forms orthodoxy. For this reason also, I am against a partialist, patchy slow adjustment approach.

The meaning of my proposition that historic formulations of Islam—juristic, theological, spiritual—can be neither ignored nor discarded consists of two parts. The first, as I just hinted above, is that if we took the Qurʾān at this point of history, as though it had been revealed just now—for that is what discarding historical Islam would mean (from this perspective, the Sunna or the performance of the Prophet himself serves, in part, as historical Islam for an understanding of the Qur'ān)—we would not be able even to understand it. Religiously speaking, no doubt, the Qur'ān has to be taken as though it were revealed to the conscience of every believer—and Sufis have sometimes taken this to an extreme—but it can be so revealed to the conscience of a believer only after it has been properly understood, which requires putting its legal and social enunciations in their historical setting. Besides, within historical Islam differences in religious attitude can be discerned, for, as I pointed out early in chapter 1, the Companions of the Prophet—his immediate audience—understood the Qur'ān and the Prophet's own performance more pragmatically than did the later generations, who increasingly became prisoners of their own principles, on the basis of which they elaborated the Qur'ānic teaching. Such early history is also involved in our understanding of Islam, not in terms of accepting all of its content but as a general pragmatic guide.

The second part of the meaning of this proposition is that we must make a thorough study, a *historically* systematic study, of the development of Islamic disciplines. This has to be primarily a critical study that will show us on the screen, as it were, the career of Islam at the hands of Muslims. But in religious terms it will be finally judged by the criterion of the Qur'ān itself—the Qur'ān as we will have understood it by the procedure described above. The need for a critical study of our intellectual Islamic past is ever more urgent because, owing to a peculiar psychological complex we have developed vis-à-vis the West, we have come to defend that past as though it were our God. Our sensitivities to the various parts or aspects of this past, of course, differ, although almost all of it has become generally sacred to us. The greatest sensitivity surrounds the Ḥadīth, although it is generally accepted that, except the Qur'ān, all else is liable to the corrupting hand of history. Indeed, a critique of Ḥadīth should not only remove a big mental block but should promote fresh thinking about Islam. Further, if a certain ḥadīth is shown to be historically unsound, it need not be discarded, for it may contain a good princple, and a good principle, no matter where it comes from, should be adopted. This is not the place to go into details, which I have elaborated in chapter 2 of my *Islamic Methodology in History* (Karachi, 1965). In the following subsection I shall endeavor to elucidate the meaning of the term "Sunna of the Prophet" and to show how this concept should be interpreted.

With regard to law, jurisprudence, theology (kalām), Sufism, philosophy, and science, fuller histories of their origin and development need to be written. Muslims have given more attention to the history of their literatures than to a historical study of these branches of their intellectual life. Recently Muslims have made some effort at producing materials for the historical development of philosophy and science, but this endeavor is still in its infancy and, particularly so far as science is concerned, is more propagandistic than scholarly and critical. Western scholarship has produced some good works in these fields, but they have barely scratched the surface. In philosophy, Western scholarship has come out with some excellent monographs and also with certain histories, which, however, treat the subject in a truncated maner, for they have assumed that whatever worthwhile Islamic philosophy there was ended with Ibn Rushd—whence it passed into the stream of Western medieval philosophy through Latin translations—which is a capital mistake. A basic difficulty with this kind of study is that it requires highly complicated and sophisticated intellectual and linguistic equipment: not only is a thorough knowledge of Greek and modern philosophy or science, or both, required, but a high intellectual caliber is needed as well.

One might ask the justification or relevance of a historical study of philosophy and science for Islamic studies, since these are apparently "secular" disciplines. The answer is that Muslim philosophers and scientists, by and large, did regard their inquiries as in a definite sense Islamic pursuits. There is no doubt that Muslim scientists were encouraged in their work by the high positive value that the Qurʾān recurrently and explicitly attaches to all knowledge, and particularly to the study of the universe. Undoubtedly, the Qurʾān has a special point of view on the ultimate nature of studies of the universe (as it has on the studies of man and history), but the fact that it encourages these studies is important. As such, they are to be regarded in general as an integral part of Islamic intellectualism. As for philosophy, although several of the findings of al-Fārābī, Ibn Sīnā, and Ibn Rushd were rejected by Muslim orthodoxy as gravely heretical, the mere fact that philosophic thought impinged so heavily on orthodox religious thought is eloquent testimony to its religious importance. And, of course, the philosophers themselves certainly regarded their intellectual effort as Islamic—indeed, as deeply religious. There is dire need for a study of this philosophical movement both as it impinged on the Islamic orthodoxy and in terms of how far the judgment passed by the orthodoxy upon it is fair, that is, to what extent the criteria of Islamic orthodoxy conform to the criteria of the Qur'ān.

One curious aspect of the history of Islamic education and intellectual life is the relative position of philosophy and Sufism vis-à-vis the orthodox system. Many forms of Sufism have been quite acceptable to the orthodoxy, and numerous Sufi shaykhs have been regarded by it as examples of piety and virtue. Yet Sufi works have hardly even been part, let alone a regular part, of the orthodox system of education; only very rarely have certain works of Ibn ʿArabī and his school of thought—a school regarded by many, perhaps most, orthodox as extremely heretical—been taught at madrasas. Philosophy, on the other hand, although several of its tenets and doctrines were vehemently rejected as heretical, did form part of the regular curriculum at most madrasas, even in Sunni Islam (except in the Arab world, where it was exorcised about the sixteenth century), though, except in Iran, its level of originality fell in the age of the great commentaries. The reason perhaps is that, for the orthodoxy, Sufism was not so much an intellectual discipline as a moral-spiritual one, so that, although many ulema cultivated Sufism and enrolled in Sufi orders for character building and practical piety, they looked upon Sufism as outside the intellectual or academic curriculum. By such madrasas as did not consider such doctines unorthodox, the works of Ibn ʿArabī and his followers were regarded as essentially intellectual products inculcating a certain intellectual world view.

So far as law, jurisprudence (called *uṣūl al-fiqh*—principles of law), and theology are concerned, the last has been treated by several modern scholars, particularly in the West, although no history of theology in Islam has so far been attempted. The early development of theological speculation in Islam and the rise and character of early schools is still obscure, chiefly owing to the paucity of original materials available. Nevertheless, very recently some Western scholars have made new contributions to our knowledge of this area. For the later period (tenth century onward) there are still many important works that lie unpublished. This only shows the lack of historical perspective from which Muslim scholarship has suffered and hence the lack of insight into the historical development of Islam. Law, again, has been treated by a number of scholars, both Western and, more recently, Muslim. The only history of Islamic law, sketchy though it is, is by N. J. Coulson, and a solid and detailed history of legal development must await a treatment of the vast field of this literature that is either unpublished or untreated. A history of Islamic law is much more difficult to essay than a history of Islamic theology, because of both the variety and the vastness of legal literature in Islam. Indeed, little is known beyond the barest outlines of the most salient doctrines of different legal schools. But far more neglected and desperate than any field of Islamic learning is the situation of the principles of law or Islamic jurisprudence. Even a cursory acquaintance with this literature from the various schools cannot fail to impress one with its originality and richness. Irrespective of how far one would consider it today to reflect the purposes of the Qurʾān, in itself it undoubtedly constitutes the highest and most authentic expression of historic Islam. Without appreciating or evaluating the juristic literature of Islam, it is impossible to evaluate the performance of historical Islam.

Apart from the usual difficulties inherent in the study of a technical literature, particularly jurisprudence, two factors appear to have discouraged scholars from undertaking a systematic and comprehensive historical study of Islamic theology and law. One is that all theological and juristic works, once the basic framework of doctrinal ideas in each field was formulated and settled, appear superficially to be little more than repetitions. For theology, particularly the main school, the Ashʿarite, although important individual writers do make their contributions, this is more or less the case, but it is certainly not true of jurisprudence. The basic framework of the "roots of law"—the Qurʾān, the Prophetic example, qiyās, or ijtihād, and ijmāʿ (consensus)—has, as demonstrated by various prominent jurists of Islam, a surprising range and richness of interpretation. And, although in the later medieval period there is a certain tendency to emphasize uniformity and even to project it backward, this artificial trend cannot eliminate the variety and should not be allowed to discourage fuller investigation. The second factor is the uninviting character of the literature of the commentaries and supercommentaries on theological and legal compendiums (but not juristic works). Now, as I said in chapter 1, this is largely a dreary field of literature, devoted mostly to hair-splitting and basically unoriginal details, but one must not suppose that it is all *repetition,* for there is a good deal of acuteness of mind displayed therein, and one can still hit upon pearls even in these stagnant waters.

Although the main work up till now in the historical treatment of Islam and Islamic disciplines has been done by Western scholars, since they have developed better methods and tools, it is undoubtedly a task that devolves primarily upon Muslims themselves. For one thing, the thoroughness and comprehensiveness required call for a massive effort, and the West cannot be expected to make such a large-scale investment. Second, it is Muslims who require this historical study so they can further assess the value of these historical developments in order to reconstruct Islamic disciplines for the future. It is not the task of Western (non-Muslim) scholars to carry out this undertaking. But the state of Muslim scholarship is, generally speaking, so poor that it is at times disheartening. Although there has been a good deal of progress in editing original texts in the Middle East, the level of intellectual life in the Islamic field is generally pitiable. In the subcontinent, where better intellectual quality is perhaps available, a sober historical scholarship that would anchor it meaningfully and reliably is lacking, with a resultant lack of intellectual discipline. In Indonesia, where Islamic scholarship has made good headway since the beginning of this century but naturally has been essentially imitating Cairo, it will be still some time before a "take-off" stage is reached. It is too early to tell, but the signs in terms of output since the mid-century are encouraging; what is necessary is to guard against such politicoreligious involvements as might precipitate the deliberate and premature creation of a peculiar Indonesian Islam, exploiting Abangan Islam as a ready-made base. Such an artificial creation would be truncated both in scholarship and in intellectualism.

Systematic Reconstruction

Theology. A historical critique of theological developments in Islam is the first step toward a reconstruction of Islamic theology. This critique, as I said before, should reveal the extent of the dislocation between the world view of the Qurʾān and various schools of theological speculation in Islam and point the way toward a new theology. Leaving aside the various extravagant speculative theological doctrines of the Bāṭinīs (Muslim esotericists) and many Sufis, the opposing schools of "rational" (Muʿtazilite) and "traditionalist" (the Ashʿarite) theology teach a student an effective lesson on this highly sensitive issue. While admitting that all theological formulations necessarily carry on their brows the dust of time, one still must demand that such formulations be faithful at least to the basic structure of ideas of the religion they claim to represent. But who would claim that the Muʿtazilite doctrines of the negation of attributes of God, of the necessity of excluding God's power from the sphere of human actions and limiting it to the realm of nature, of denial of God's forgiveness of sins, are faithful to the teaching of the Qurʾān? And, even more so, who can claim that the Ashʿarite reaction in terms of the doctrines of the omnipotence of God at the expense of all human power and will, of the purposelessness of divine commands and prohibitions, of making works essentially irrelevant to faith, of the denial of cause and effect, and, consequently, the elevation of atomism to the position of a cardinal principle of the Islamic creed was representative of the Qurʾānic teaching on God, man, or nature? A system of theology may be logically coherent yet totally false to the religion it claims to formulate, for what can one say of a theological system that reigned supreme in the greater part of the Islamic world for the best part of a millennium and whose votaries—some of them august names in the history of Islamic thought like al-Ghazālī and al-Rāzī—vied with one another in producing ever fresh arguments to prove that man can be said "to act" only metaphysically, not really, since the only real "actor" is God?

It is to the credit of premodernist revivalism and modernism that they tried to undermine this thousand-year-old sacred folly and to invite Muslims back to the refreshing fountain of the Qurʾān. But whereas premodernist fundamentalism was good at demolishing the choking prison and letting in fresh air, it refused to build any new edifice. Rather, it believed that all edifices are really prisons, or inevitably become so, and that religion is better off without a theology, which in its eyes amounted to a crime against religion. As for modernism, it has, for the most part, dealt with matters social and political issue-by-issue, not as a social or political philosophy. Democracy is Islamic, but concepts like human rights and social justice (which are certainly declared to be Islamic) are not much discussed; egalitarianism is emphasized, but its nature and limits, if any, do not come up as problems; Islam has given women rights, but why and what kinds of rights and by what rationale are not clear. Most modernists are very reticent about a theology, a philosophy, a world view. In Muḥammad ʿAbduh's work theology is minimal, although he did much to resurrect Muʿtazila-type rationalism; Sayyid Aḥmad Khān called desperately for a new kalām (theology) consonant with the requirements of the age and felt sure that, unless theology was reformulated afresh, Islam would be in real and grave danger—like all other religions. At his instance, Muḥammad Shiblī wrote two books in Urdu—a history of theology in Islam called *ʿIlm al-Kalām,* and a systematic theology called *Kalām*—wherein he attempted to restate arguments for God's existence, prophethood, revelation, and such, relying heavily, like Sayyid Aḥmad Khān himself, upon medieval Muslim philosophers like Ibn Sīnā.

It was the philosopher-poet Muḥammad Iqbāl who essayed a new approach to Islamic theology in his *Reconstruction of Religious Thought in Islam.* Iqbāl was a keen student of modern Western philosophy as well as of Islamic mysticism (essentially in Persian), but he was not a scholar of the Islamic theological tradition or of the Qurʾān (which, however, he read a great deal for inspiration). Iqbāl appears to me to have very rightly perceived that the basic impulse of the Qurʾān was dynamic and action oriented—seeking to direct history on a spiritual value pattern and attempting to create a world order. As I said earlier, I do not accept the judgment of the late H. A. R. Gibb that one cannot consider Iqbal's work even as a point of departure for building a new Islamic theology; it seems to me that Gibb was probably thinking in terms of a new system of Islamic *credal formulae.* It is, however, correct to say that Iqbāl's attempt is very much dated, since he took seriously his contemporary scientists who tried to prove a dynamic free will in man on the basis of the new subatomic scientific data, which they interpreted as meaning that the physical world was "free" of the chain of cause and effect! It is true too that Iqbāl did not carry out any systematic inquiry into the teaching of the Qurʾān but picked and chose from its verses—as he did with other traditional material—to prove certain theses at least some of which were the result of his general insight into the Qur'ān but which, above all, seemed to him to suit most the contemporary needs of a stagnant Muslim society. He then expressed these theses in terms of such contemporary evolutionary theories as those of Bergson and Whitehead. My disagreement with Iqbāl is therefore not over his concept of God—as the ultimate source of creative energy that can be appropriated by individuals and societies in certain ways—but with his formulation of this concept and the method by which he attempts to deduce it from the Qur'ān.

This account further demonstrates the necessity of the procedure I have advocated for a systematic interpretation of the Qur'ān. For the theological or metaphysical statements of the Qur'ān, the specific revelational background is not necessary, as it is for its social-legal pronouncements, nor do the commentators usually give it, but certainly without a systematic study the Qur'ānic world view cannot emerge. It cannot be denied that any such interpretation will necessarily be influenced by contemporary modes of thought; this is also required in the sense that only in this way can the message of the Qur'ān become relevant to the contemporary situation. But it is quite another thing to couch the Qur'ānic message in terms of a particular theory, no matter how attractive, sensational, or popular it may seem—in fact, the more topical a theory is, the less suitable it is as a vehicle of expression of an eternal message. It is also possible that this is what Gibb meant by his critique of Iqbāl, but then it is possible to separate Iqbāl's basic insights into the nature of Islam from the doctrines in terms of which he has formulated them.

Law and ethics. Muslim scholars have never attempted an ethics of the Qur'ān, systematically or otherwise. Yet no one who has done any careful study of the Qur'ān can fail to be impressed by its ethical fervor. Its ethics, indeed, is its essence, and it is also the necessary link between theology and law. It is true that the Qur'ān tends to concretize the ethical, to clothe the general in a particular paradigm, and to translate the ethical into legal or quasi-legal commands. But it is precisely a sign of its moral fervor that it is not content only with generalizable ethical propositions but is keen on translating them into actual paradigms. However, as I have repeatedly pointed out, the Qur'ān always explicates the objectives or principles that are the essence of its laws.

The Muslims' failure to make a clear distinction between Qur'ānic ethics and law has resulted in a confusion between the two. Neither ethics nor law ever became a discipline in itself. Islamic law, in fact, is not law in a modern sense; it is a treasure of legal materials thrown up during long centuries of endless discussions, upon which modern Islamic legal systems can certainly be built, but only a part of which could ever be enforced in court. No doubt the mixing together of law and morality gave a certain character to Islamic law that is uniquely precious—namely, it kept the moral motivation, without which any law must become a plaything of legal tricksters and manipulators, alive within the law. However, to keep law permeated with a living moral sense it is not necessary to ignore the distinction between the two, only to keep law *organically* relatd to morality, that is, to keep law Islamic and prevent its secularization.

The Qurʾān calls itself "guidance for mankind" (*hudan liʾl-nās*) and by the same term designates earlier revealed documents. Its central moral concept for man in *taqwā*, which is usually translated as "piety" or "God-fearingness" but which in the various Qurʾānic contexts may be defined as "a mental state of responsibility from which an agent's actions proceed but which recognizes that the criterion of judgment upon them lies outside him." The whole business of the Qurʾān appears to be centered on the attempt to induce such a state in man. The idea of a secular law, insofar as it makes this state indifferent to its obedience, which is consequently conceived in mechanical terms, is the very abnegation of taqwā. The increasingly chaotic state of affairs in Western societies and the gradual erosion of an inner sense of responsibility represent a complex situation, but this situation is undoubtedly linked with a process through which law ceased to maintain any organic relation to morality.

Nor is Islamic theology, for that matter, a case of pure intellectualism, unaffective and ineffective, a pure artificial construct that tries to vie with philosophy, which at least claims to start from assumptions of natural reason rather than from given dogmatic beliefs that it claims "to prove." Islamic theology is certainly an intellectual endeavor, but it is so in the sense that it gives a coherent and faithful account of what is there in the Qurʾān so that a believing person or a person prone to believe can give consent both from the mind and from the heart and make this world view his or her mental and spiritual home. Insofar as it provides that intellectual home for the mind, it can be taught; insofar as it provides a spiritual haven for the heart, it can be preached. A theology that can perform neither of these two functions is the stark bone of religion. Al-Ghazālī had long ago condemned the official "science of theology" because it was neither spiritually satisfying nor intellectually satisfactory—he called it the game of intellectual children! Yet this seems to be the fate of most historical theologies.

Just as preaching is an expression of theology for the heart, even so must it give rise to morality or an ethical value system to guide man and to instill in him the sense of moral responsibility that the Qur'ān calls taqwā. A God that speaks neither to the intellect of man nor to his heart, nor yet can generate a system of values for man, is considerably worse than nothing and is better off dead. The moral values are the crucial pivot of the entire overall system, and from them flows the law. The law is therefore the last part in this chain and governs all the "religious," social, political, and economic institutions of the society. Because law is to be formulated on the basis of the moral values, it will necessarily be organically related to the latter. But because it governs the day-to-day life of the society, with necessary social change it has to be reinterpreted. Should the process of reinterpretation stop, obviously the society must either stagnate or else rebel and take the road of secularism. In either case the whole structure of theology, morality, and law will eventually collapse.

The question of who should interpret law has been acute in Islamic societies because of the historical accident that the so-called law (fiqh) has been the result of the work of private lawyers, while in the later medieval centuries governments—particularly the Ottoman government—had to promulgate laws on issues not covered by the Sharīʿa law. Although the state-made law was basically sanctioned by certain general principles in the Sharīʿa law itself, nevertheless a dichotomy of the sources of law was unavoidable, and this process paved the way for the secularization of law in several Muslim countries—most systematically in Turkey. With the introduction of parliamentary institutions, law-making has become the business of lay parliamentarians, but there are large-scale protests from the ulema and their supporters that law-making must be vested in the ulema institutions. For centuries, however, law-making in the ulema institutions has been stagnant, and it is no longer feasible to reverse the new arrangements. The only way to produce genuine Islamic law is to enlighten public conscience, particularly that of the educated classes, with Islamic values. This, in fact, underlines the necessity of working out Islamic ethics systematically from the Qur᾿ān and making such works accessible to the general reader. There is no shortcut to this process for the production of Islamic law. There is no doubt that a wider study of earlier works of Islamic jurisprudence and law will help. If first-rate works on the history of Islamic law and jurisprudence are written—as I have argued must be done—these should be made required reading in the schools of law as part of the normal curriculum. In this way, key Islamic legal and moral concepts would gradually come to inform the legal profession. In many Muslim countries the lawyers themselves are keen to learn more about Islamic law. Perhaps an international committee of Muslim jurists could be organized with first-rate traditionalist scholars of law and jurisprudence of various medieval schools to undertake major works in the field. At present, al-Azhar happens to be the most hopeful center for such a development.

Philosophy. In medieval Islam, a series of brilliant and original men had built, on the basis of Greek philosophical thought, a comprehensive and sysematic view of the universe and of man, which they were able to synthesize with certain key concepts and doctrines of Islam to the satisfaction of themselves and many of the sophisticated Muslim intelligentsia. As I said earlier, this body of thought, called philosophy (*al-falsafa*), gave violent affront to the orthodoxy on several issues, and since then philosophy has been a disciplina non grata in the Muslim educational system throughout a large part of the Muslim world. As I pointed out earlier, this was only one type of philosophy, with which nevertheless the fate of all philosophy was bound up in the eyes of the orthodox, and this circumstance caused a great deal of harm both to the orthodoxy (which suffered from a lack of ideas and their challenge) and to philosophy. Philosophy did continue to be cultivated at a high level in Iran, but this was done away from the orthodox fold—and even the Shīʿī orthodox fold—and therefore the two hardly ever met. Philosophy is, however, a perennial intellectual need and has to be allowed to flourish both for its own sake and for the sake of other disciplines, since it inculcates a much-needed analytical-critical spirit and generates new ideas that become important intellectual tools for other sciences, not least for religion and theology. Therefore a people that deprives itself of philosophy necessarily exposes itself to starvation in terms of fresh ideas—in fact, it commits intellectual suicide.

The generation of ideas by philosophy is basically a function of its critical-analytical activity. This activity has to be free. Most probably, philosophy as such cannot create any beliefs about reality and its nature, since its function is to analyze data of experience—sense experience, aesthetic experience, or religious experience. Philosophy, therefore, is not a rival of theology but should be helpful to it, for the object of the latter is to build a world view on the basis of the Qur'ān with the help of the intellectual tools provided, in part, by philosophy. Certain philosophical views may create tensions with certain theological doctrines; in this case either that particular philosophical view may be Islamically questionable or it may be that a particular theological doctrine is questionable. In any case, possible or actual tensions are not an excuse for banning philosophy in the name of a self-righteous theology, or vice versa: I have said already, and my argument has assumed all along in this work, that difference of opinion, provided it is meaningful, has to be assigned a high positive value, for it is only through confrontation of different and opposing views that truth *gradually* emerges. In fact, there is no privileged point in the process of human thought where *the Truth* can be said to have dawned.

Because medieval Muslim philosophy was a particular type of philosophical system, one must ask whether it is correct or wise to ban all philosophy (al-falsafa) as such. There can be any number of philosophies depending on point of view, the assumptions a particular philosopher makes, and the problems he starts out to solve, namely, those that seem to him to be most important, whether in the field of metaphysics, or ethics, or epistemology, or logic, or whatever. To say that all philosophy must of necessity contradict theology or its suppositions is to play not only a naive game but a dangerous one. I can say without fear of contradiction that, for the Qur'ān, knowledge—that is, the creation of ideas—is an activity of the highest possible value. Otherwise why did it ask the Prophet to continue to pray for "increase in knowledge"? Why did it untiringly emphasize delving into the universe, into history, and into man's own inner life? Is the banning or discouragement of pure thought compatible with this kind of demand? What does Islam have to fear from human thought and why? These are questions that must be answered by those "friends of religion" who want to keep their religion in a hothouse, secluded from the open air.

The social sciences. Social sciences, as systematized bodies of knowledge, that is, as disciplines, are a modern phenomenon. They are undoubtedly a very important development, since, the object of their study being man in society, they can tell us so much about how collectivities actually behave in various fields of human belief and action. At the begining of this chapter I said something about Muslims' desire to Islamize these sciences or bodies of knowledge. There is no doubt that here again the vicious circle I have repeatedly spoken of can be broken only at the level of an intellectual activity where works are produced not only to inform how societies actually behave but to show how they can be imbued with Islamic values conducive to the establishment of an ethical social order in the world.

As a system of values, Islam naturally cannot favor a laissez-faire society. On the other hand, Islam knows well that coercion does not pay or even work. As for indoctrination in the sense of brainwashing, I have already pointed out that this technique of creating future generations of the faithful in fact ultimately backfires. If in the past social pressures helped indoctrination in the sense that people rarely rebelled openly, this situation is increasingly changing, since social pressures are weakening and, owing to a number of apparently irreversible factors, are bound to continue to weaken. In fact, an intense and irrational faith in a subjective humanism among several present-day "liberated" circles has led many to "leave our chidlren alone when they are young so that they can choose their own way of life when they are adults" and the like. Such statements, often made in good faith (although at least as often they are merely a cheap cover for disowning parental responsibility), in fact betray a lack of concern for the future of humanity. For, if humans could grow by themselves, highly sophisticated religious and educational systems would not have developed in the first place. And what we are seeing develop in societies whose liberals think they are the first secular liberals in human history is that, instead of growing into humans, many of the new generation are in fact growing into animals. To remedy the crudity and even cruelty of a self-righteous traditional system is one thing. To throw out the baby with the bath water is quite another.

Indoctrination, however, necessarily occurs only where dogmas come in: the greater the dogma content, the greater the need for indoctrination; the greater the ethical content, the less the need for indoctrination. It is a pity of pities that the ethical content of societies is being washed out because of a general rebellion against dogmas. Dogmas, again, are not all of the same level, for there are relatively "rational" dogmas, that is, such as are tied to the ethical content of a system. In any case, universal ethical values are the crux of the being of a society: the debate about the relativity of moral values in societies is born of a liberalism that in the process of liberalization has become so perverted as to destroy those very moral values it set out to liberate from the constraints of dogma. From my point of view, which is confessedly and necessarily normative, therefore, the best of social sciences is history—if done well and objectively. This is because history, being long range, contains lessons in a way that a study of the contemporary aborigines of Australia, for example, does not. Macrohistory, if done really well, is the best service a social scientist can do for mankind. This is the reason the Qur'ān invites us again and again "to travel on the earth and see the end of nations." Microhistory—for example, a study of the postal service in the United States in the 1850s, is of use only insofar as it contributes to our knowledge of the behavior of man and its consequences; otherwise it is pure curiosity or a means to securing an academic post in a modern institution of learning.

Modern societies have acquired far more complexity than ancient and medieval societies. Particularly in the fields of economics, politics, communication, and education, modern societies have evolved thought, institutions, and structures incomparably more complex and sophisticated than those of any society within human experience. Yet we must not be deluded into thinking that because of their sophistication and complexity modern societies are any less subject to the basic laws of right and wrong. Part of modern sophistication, in fact, means that these societies have become more aware, or at least have the means to become more aware, of the possible sources of such social dislocations as might threaten to derange them. All such dislocations are finally rooted in the sense of right and wrong that is the conscience of the social mind. But it is always touch and go whether the conscience of a given social mind does in fact manage to reflect right and wrong with adequate objectivity. Since modern societies are, then, subject to the laws of rights and wrong just as were earlier, and in many ways simpler, societies, the lessons of history are as relevant to them as they were to the earlier ones. But, despite the increasingly sophisticated warning systems of today, the ethical impulse in certain important respects seems to have become, if anything, weaker. It is true that earlier societies were much more dogmatic in certain respects and therefore exposed themselves to dangers, while modern sophistication means less dogmatism, overtly at least. But this competence of modern societies to adjust to necessary change is often like a doctor who treats symptoms rather than the disease. No matter how much a doctor gains competence in treating symptoms while ignoring or being ignorant of the underlying disease, the life of his patient cannot be much prolonged. It is to be feared that modern civilization, while sophisticating means and methods to almost no end, has developed cardinal deficiencies in basic insights into human nature.

It is therefore essential that social scientists who study contemporary societies be exposed to the sobering lessons of history, for the history of mankind, whether earlier societies were aware of this or not, is indivisible in the sense that the basic human forces—and it is the human forces that are basic to history—are the same all over the globe. This is certainly the view of the Qurʾān, which is singularly free of genetics and genes. If Muslim social scientists are to be involved in social engineering, this is all the more necessary. There is a considerable body of what may be called social thought in the Qurʾān, which talks incessantly about the rise and fall of societies and civilizations, of the moral decrepitude of nations, of the succession of civilizations or "the inheritance of the earth," of the function of leadership, of prosperity and peace and their opposites, and especially of "those who sow corruption on the earth but think they are reformers." This body of thought should be organized next to the pure moral thought of the Qurʾān and the lessons from history upon which the Qurʾān is so insistent. Unless the material of the Qurʾān is well systematized, it can be dangerously misleading to apply individual and isolated verses to situations, as most Muslim preachers and even many intellectuals tend to do.

The views of the Qurʾān will also remain at the level of pure abstraction unless a thorough *factual* survey is made of the relevant social data. It is of the greatest importance to determine exactly where society is at present before deciding where it can go. To talk about reforming society without scientifically determining where the society is, is certainly like a doctor treating a patient without taking his case history or examining him. In fact, there is a sense in which even a meaningful formulation of Qurʾānic thought will be dependent upon such a factual study and a proper method for interpreting facts; the converse, as I underlined in the Introduction, is also true. In other words, as with other fields discussed above, the study of the social sciences is a process, not something that is established once and for all. In fact, it is more so than any other field, for its subject matter—social behavior—is constantly in the process of creation.

Index

ʿAbbās II, 66
ʿAbduh, Muḥammad, 69–70, 82, 85; and al-Azhar, 64–65, 66–67, 68, 98–100, 130; on education, 60, 63, 77, 90; on science, 49–51, 55; on theology, 153
Ạbdul Hamīd II, 69
Adultery, 30, 31
Afghānī, Jamāl al-Dīn al-, 49–51, 64
Ahl-i-Ḥadīth school, 41–42
Aḥmad, Nadhr, 40
Aḥmadiya sect, 123
Aḥmad Khān, Sayyid, 54, 60, 62, 70, 72, 85; and Aligarh college, 52, 74, 78, 79; on education of women, 77; on historic Islam, 120; and Muslim Educational Conference, 76; on science and theology, 49–52, 55–56, 153
Akhavi, Shahrough, 106
Akhbārīs, 107
Akhlāq-i-Jalālī, 52
Akhlāq-i-Nāsirī, 52
Alfiya (Ibn Mālik), 37
Algeria, 44
ʿAlī, 24
ʿAlī, Muḥammad, 59, 63, 64
Aligarh Muslim college, 52, 56, 72, 74, 75, 78, 79, 115
ʿAlī Khān, Osman, 75, 76
ʿAlī Khān, Ẓafar, 72
ʿĀlimiya, al-, 64
Allāhābādī, Akbar, 72
Amīr ʿAlī, Sayyid, 49–51, 53
Analogical reasoning. *See* Qiyās
Anbābī, Muḥammad al-, 64, 67, 68
Anglo-Iranian Oil Company, 105
Ankara University, 92–93, 94–96, 103, 108
Apologetic literature, 4, 96, 103, 133
Aquinas, 10
Arabia, 6, 43–44, 133
Arabic grammar, 36, 37, 40
Arabic language, 38, 78, 95, 97, 119, 126, 127, 138
Arabic literature, 36, 40
Arabs, and custom, 17–18
Arberry, A. J., 144
Aristotle, 38
Ashʿarī, al-, 10
Ashʿarism, 3, 70; development of, 26–27; and metaphysics, 132–33; and Qurʾān, 152
Ash-Shiddiqy, Hasbi, 128

Asian Drama (Myrdal), 28, 88
Assembly of Islamic Scholars. *See* Nadwat al-ʿUlamāʾ; Nahḍat al-ʿUlamāʾ
Association for a Religious Monthly, 107
Astronomy, 35, 40, 48, 67, 135
Atatürk, Kemāl, 53, 54, 62, 63, 70, 85, 91, 92, 94, 95, 140, 146
Atatürk University, 93, 96
Atay, Husayin, 92n
Atomism, 27, 152
Augustine, 10, 11
Ayūb Khān, Muḥammad, 118, 122, 123, 125
Ayyubids, 31
Āzād, Abūʾl-Kalām, 72
Azhar, al-, 31, 69–70, 78–79, 80, 113, 122, 130, 157; and Indonesia, 126–27, 128–29; medieval curriculum of, 36–37; modernization of, 98–104, 138–39; reform of, 63–68

"Bahs-i Dar Bāreh-yi Marjiʿiyat wa Ruhāniyat," 107–8
Balance of Truth (Khalīfa), 34
Baltacioğlu, Ismail Hakki, 54, 61, 94
Bāqillānī, al-, 27
Bāqir Mīr Dāmād, Muḥammad, 35–36
Barelavī school, 41–42
Barnes, G. D., 111
Bāṭinīs, 143, 152
Baydawī, al-, 36
Bāzargān, 109
Bell, Richard, 103
Bergson, Henri, 154
Berkes, Niyazi, 48n, 61
Betti, E., 8–9
Bhutto, Z. A., 114, 118
Bihishtī Zewar (Thānavī), 76–77
Board of Useful Affairs, 48
Book of Scholarship and Scholars, The (al-Zawāhirī), 64–65
Bradley, F. H., 132
British, 43, 44, 54, 110, 119; in Egypt, 79–80; in India, 44, 57, 59–60, 72, 75, 79–80; in Iran, 79–80, 105
Burūjirdī, 107

Caliphate, destruction of, 26, 27, 29
Causality, 27, 32, 152
Central Institute of Islamic Research, 123
Charlemagne, 16
China, Peoples' Republic of, 114
Christianity, 5, 54, 120; compared with Islam, 98, 124; dualism of, 58; and effective history, 10; theology of, 14–15
Classical modernism, 43–83; and contemporary modernism, 85; and fundamentalism, 136–37, 142–43; in Egypt, 59–61, 63–68, 77, 82; in India, 59, 62, 72–79, 81; in Indonesia, 81–83; in Iran, 79–81; and theology, 152–53; in Turkey, 47–49, 59–60, 61–63, 77, 78. *See also* Islamic education
Colonialism, 4, 50, 63; and course of modernization, 43–45, 59; educational systems of, 57, 59–61, 89, 112; and Islamic revival, 54–55, 71–72. *See also* West
Commentaries and supercommentaries on Qurʾān, 17, 36–39, 40, 45, 63, 70, 103, 128, 145, 150–51
Companions of the Prophet, 17, 23–24, 31, 144, 147
Consensus. *See* Ijmāʿ
Contemporary modernism, 84–129; and classical modernism, 85; in Egypt, 85, 87, 98–104, 138–39; in Indonesia, 97–98, 138; in Iran, 104–9; in Turkey, 85, 90, 91, 92–99, 104, 126, 138–39. *See also* Islamic education
Coulson, N. J., 150

Criterion of Actions (al-Ghazālī), 34–35

Dā'irat al-Ma'ārif, 76
Dār al-Funūn, 69
Dār al-Qāda', 66, 68
Dār al-'Ulūm, 130
Dars-i-Niẓāmī, 40–41
Dawn, 123
Democracy, 88, 89, 114, 118, 136, 139–40, 152–53
Deoband seminary, 41–42, 56, 74, 76, 78, 79, 82, 115
"Deserted Village, The" (Goldsmith), 28
Dictionary of Technical Terms (al-Tahānavī), 37
Disputation, 37
Dogma, 160, 161
Dogmatic method in hermeneutics, 10–11
Dutch, 43, 44

Economic development, 87–89
Education Conference of 1947 (Pakistan), 110, 112
"Effective eccentrics," 61
Effective history, 9–11
Egypt, 23, 83, 95–96, 105, 130; and classical modernism, 59–61, 63–68, 77, 82; and contemporary modernism, 85, 87, 98–104, 138–39; Islamic thought in, 113; medieval education in, 31, 36–37; premodernist, 44, 45; ulema in, 44–45, 63, 79–80, 98, 103–4. *See also* Azhar, al-
Engineering, 48, 113
English language instruction, 75, 78, 115
Ethics, 154–57

Faith: and science, 51; and understanding, 4–5, 132, 134–35
Falsafa, al-. *See* Philosophy
Fārābī, al-, 34, 96, 148
Farāhī, Ḥamīd al-Dīn al-, 78
Fatherland, The (Namik Kemāl), 53
Fatimids, 31
Fawz al-Kabīr fī uṣūl a-Tafsīr, al-, (Walīy Allāh), 40
Fayẓī, 37
Fikret, Tevfik, 61–62
Fiqh, 33, 35, 67, 97. *See also* Islamic law
Firangī Maḥal madrasa, 40, 78
Five Pillars, 19, 30–31, 116
Freedom, and Islamic thought, 125
Free will, 3, 27, 33, 70, 100, 152, 153
French, 43, 44, 48, 49
Fundamentalism, 136, 141–43, 152. *See also* Neorevivalism (neofundamentalism)
Future of Culture in Egypt, The (Tahā Husayn), 54

Gadamer, Hans Georg, 8–11
Galatasaray lycée, 61–62
Gasprinsky, Isma'il, 53
Ghazālī, al-, 3–4, 10, 99, 128; and Ash'arism, 27; on instrumental sciences, 67; and knowledge, 34–35, 135; theology of, 14, 152, 156
Gibb, H. A. R., 132–33, 153, 154
God: differing conceptions of, 144–45; as regulative idea in Islam, 14. *See also* Theology
Gökalp, Zia, 53–54, 62, 69
Goldsmith, Oliver, 28
Goldziher, Ignaz, 120
Graduation, principle of, 16
Greek thought, 3, 33, 71, 86, 132, 157
Guftār-i-Māh, 107
"Guidance of Husayn," 108

Ḥadīth, 45–46, 76, 78, 143; appeal to individual texts of, 25–26; integrity of, 21, 95, 103, 120, 147; in premodern Islam, 36, 40, 41;

sociohistorical study of, 95, 96–97
Hakīm, Abd al-, 38, 45
Ḥālī, Alṭāf Ḥusayn, 60–61, 70–71
Hamdard Islamicus, 76
Haq, Ziaul, 118
Ḥaqq, ʿAbd al-, 40
Ḥasan, Maḥmūd al-, 79
Hastings, Warren, 73–74
Ḥikmat, 80
Hillī, al-, 29, 33
Hinduism, 98, 119, 120
Hindus, 74, 79
Historical method in hermeneutics, 10–11
History, study of: critical, 120; revival of interest in, 52–53, 56; value of, 96–97, 160–62
Ḥudūd, 2, 31
Humanities, 131–32
Ḥusayn, 80
Husayn, Ṭahā, 54
"Ḥusayniya Irshād," 108–9

IAIN, 126
Ibn ʿArabī, 3–4, 27, 149
Ibn Khaldūn, 64, 67, 68, 128
Ibn Mālik, 37
Ibn Masʿud, 24
Ibn Rushd, 148
Ibn Sīnā, 3–4, 32, 34, 38, 40, 50, 96, 153
Ibn Taymiya, 3–4, 10, 29, 30, 99
Ijāza, 31
Ijmāʿ, 30, 107, 146, 150
Ijtihād, 7–8, 18, 82, 107–8, 128, 142, 150
Ikhwān, 141
ʿIlm al-Kalām (Shiblī), 153
Imām, 29, 33, 79, 105, 108–9
Imām khatīb (imām-hatip) schools, 62–63, 92–94
India, 53, 71; British in, 44, 57, 59–60, 72, 75, 79–80; and classical modernism, 59, 62, 72–79, 81; early, sciences in, 37, 39–42; Islamic scholarship in, 151; madrasas in, 40–42, 73–74; philosophy in, 35, 39–40; ulema in, 44–45, 78–80. *See also* Indo-Pakistan subcontinent
Indoctrination, 159–60
Indonesia: and classical modernism, 81–83; and contemporary modernism, 97–98, 126–27, 138; Islamic revival in, 54–55; Islamic scholarship in, 151; premodernism in, 45–46; ulema in, 44–45, 46
Indo-Pakistan subcontinent, 35, 39–42
Inheritance, 18–19
Inönü, Ismet, 63, 92
Institut Agama Islam Negeri, 126
Institute of Islamic Culture, 123
Interest, ban on. *See* Usury
"Investigation concerning Religious Authority and Religious Leadership," 107–8
Iqbāl, Muḥammad, 53, 72, 73, 116; on education, 56–58, 86, 90, 110; on Islamic history, 120; literary style of, 70–71; on metaphysics, 132–33; on theology, 153–54
Iran, 31, 70; and colonialism, 44; medieval education in, 35, 45; and modernism, 79–81, 104–9; philosophy in, 35, 45, 80, 106–7, 157; ulema in, 44, 79–81, 104–6, 108–9
Iraq, 23, 24
ʿIrfān, 45
Islamic Advisory Council (Pakistan), 108
Islamic Culture, 76
Islamic education: defensive strategy in, 86–87; dualistic attitude in, 46–47, 69, 91; expansion of intellectual vision in, 134–35; and indoctrination, 159–60; integration of old and new in, 71–73, 135–36, 138–39; and "Islamization,"

130–34; and literary reform, 70–71; low priority of, 89–91; medieval, 31–42; and Muslim modernists, 49–58; and nationalism, 49, 53–55, 87–88; and neorevivalists, 136–37; and politics, 139–40; precolonial, 43–46; primary, 48, 59–63, 68, 131; and professional training, 46–47, 89–90, 101–2, 113; "vicious circle" of, 86, 118, 139, 145, 159. *See also* Madrasas
Islamic gnosis, 45
Islamic intellectualism, defined, 1
Islamic jurisprudence, 123, 148, 150, 157
Islamic law: at al-Azhar, 99, 101, 138–39; development of, 29–31, 32; and early generations, 2, 23–25; in Iran, 107; penal, 2, 30–31; and piecemeal understanding of Islamic texts, 2–3, 25–26, 31; principle of graduation in, 16; and secular law, 29–30, 103–4, 155, 156; sociohistorical study of, 96–97, 145–46, 149–50, 157; study of, in early madrasas, 33, 35, 39, 41; systematic reconstruction of, 154–57
Islamic literature, 52, 70–71
Islamic mysticism. *See* Sufism
Islamic orthodoxy: and philosophy, 35–36, 148–49, 157; and premodernist education, 45–46; resistance to change by, 99, 100, 101, 146. *See also* Ijmāʿ; Sunnism
Islamic Research Institute, 123–25
Islamic sciences: critical history of, 145–51; in medieval madrasas, 33–37, 39, 40, 41, 74. *See also* Science
Islamic society, static quality of, 17–18, 26, 28
Islamic Studies, 76, 123
Islamic universities, 126. *See also* names of individual universities
Istanbul, University of, 93, 94

Jadal, 37
Jamāʿat-i-Islāmī, 82–83, 115–16, 117–18, 121, 122
Jāmiʿa ʿAbbasīya, 122
Jāmiʿa Milliya Islāmiya, 79
Jamʿiyat-i-Ṭalaba, 117–18
Java, 46, 82, 127
Jesus, 16
Jewelry of Paradise (Thānavī), 76–77
Jihād, 7–8, 55
Jīlānī, ʿAbd al-Qādir al-, 39
Jinnah, Muḥammad ʿAli, 110
Judgment on nations, 13–14

Kalām, 26–27, 32–33, 103. *See also* Theology
Kalām (Shiblī), 153
Kāmil, Muṣṭafā, 53
Kant, Immanuel, 14
Karachi, 42; University of, 117–18, 119, 121
Kashshāf Iṣṭlāḥat al-Funūn (al-Tahānavī), 37
Kemāl, Muṣṭafā. *See* Atatürk, Kemāl
Kemāl, Namik, 49–51, 53, 70, 77
Khaffājī, Shihāb al-Dīn al-, 36
Khālid, Muḥammad Khālid, 100
Khalīfa, Hajjī, 34
Khānqāh, 39
Khayālī, al-, 38
Khomeini, Āyatullāh, 79, 105, 107, 108, 109
Kitāb al-ʿIlm wa-al-ʿUlamā (al-Zawāhirī), 64–65
Kitāb al-Tajrīd (Nasīr al-Dīn al-Ṭūsī), 37
Knowledge: Islamic attitudes toward modern, 46–47; and Qurʾān, 34, 50–51, 52, 134–36, 158. *See also* Science; Technology

Lahore, 42, 72, 119
Lāhurī, al-, 38, 45
Last Judgment, 13–14
Law. *See* Islamic law
Law of the Unification of Education (Turkey), 62, 69, 96
Leftism, 118
Liberalism, 88, 111, 127–28, 160
Logic, 39, 40, 67
Luther, Martin, 10, 11

Macrohistory, 160
Madrasa ʿĀliya, 73–74
Madrasas: girls' education in, 77–78; in India, 40–42, 73–74; in Indonesia, 46, 126, 127; in Iran, 106; medieval, 31–39; and modernization, 47–48, 59, 61, 62, 69, 134; in Pakistan, 42, 112, 114–15, 116, 119, 121, 122, 123, 124; and philosophy, 149; precolonial, 44, 46; reformed, 74, 78–79; and Sufism, 149; in Turkey, 61, 62, 69–70, 92. *See also* Islamic education
Madrasat al-Banāt, 77
Madrasat al-Iṣlāh, 78–79
Maghrib zadah, 72
Mahdī, Muḥammad al-Abbāsī al-, 67
Mahmud II, 47–48
Majalla, 29
Manāhij al-Albāb (al-Ṭahṭāwī), 64
Marjiʿ-i-taqlīd, 107–8
Marxism, 84, 114–15
Materialism, 57–58, 89
Mathematics, 35, 48, 67, 68, 135
Mathnavī (Rūmī), 39, 57–58
Māturīdī, al-, 27, 32
Mawdūdī, Abū'l-Aʿla, 72, 116, 117, 118
Mecca, 13–14, 16, 17, 45–46, 82, 134
Medina, 14, 16, 82
Mehmet Fātih, 35
Metaphysics, 3, 34, 132, 154. *See also* Philosophy
Microhistory, 160
Min Hunā Nabdaʾ (Khālid), 100
Mīzān al-ʿAmal (al-Ghazālī), 34–35
Mīzān al-Ḥaqq (Khalīfa), 34
Monthly Speeches, 107
Muḥaddith, 40
Muḥammad, the Prophet, 1–2, 8, 31, 41, 103, 134, 141, 158; gradualism of reforms by, 17–18; and revelation, 16, 17–18; and social morality, 13–14, 15–17, 116–17
Muḥammad (Mehmet) the Conqueror, madrasa of, 69
Muḥammadiya reformist group, 46, 82–83, 125, 126, 128
Mujtahid, 100
Mullā Sadrā, 35–36, 39
Muqaddima (Ibn Khaldūn), 64, 67, 68
Murder, 144
Musaddas (Ḥālī), 60–61, 71, 72
Muslim Brotherhood, 116–17
Muslim Educational Conference, 76
Mustaqbal al-thaqāfa fī Miṣr (Tahā Husayn), 54
Muṭahharī, Murtazā, 108
Muʿtazila, 36, 107, 133; free will doctrine of, 33; and Muslim modernists, 51, 52, 67, 100, 153; and Qurʾān, 152
Myrdal, Gunnar, 28, 88

Nadvī, Abu'l-ḤasanʿAli al-, 78
Nadvī, Sayyid Sulaymān, 120
Nadwat al-ʿUlamāʾ, 56, 78, 115
Nahḍat al-ʿUlamāʾ, 46, 82–83, 125, 128
Nasafī, al-, 32, 38
Naṣir, Muḥammad, 82
Naṣṣ, 25
Nationalism, 49, 53–55, 87–88
National Islamic University, 79, 82–83
Nationalization, 88
Natsir, 82

Neorevivalism (neofundamentalism), 136–37, 142. *See also* Fundamentalism
Nigeria, 44
Niẓām al-Dīn, Mullā, 40, 41
Niẓāmī curriculum, 40–41
North Africa, 44
Nūr Khān, Muḥammad, 115

"Objectivity school" in hermeneutics, 8–9
Organization of Awqāf, 104
Oriental College, 119, 122
Orientalists, 95, 120, 124
Original thought. *See* Ijtihād
Origins of Muhammedan Jurisprudence (Schacht), 24
Osmania University, 75–76
Ottoman language and history, 95
Ottomans, 29, 35, 48, 49, 59, 156
Oxford University, 120, 121

Pakistan, 45, 58, 74, 98; divided culture of, 75–76; failure of Islamic education in, 110–25; Islamic Advisory Council, 108; Islamic Research Institute, 123–25; Jamāʿat-i-Islāmī in, 82–83, 115–16, 117–18, 121, 122; madrasas in, 42, 112, 114–15, 116, 119, 121, 122, 123, 124; public sector education in, 118–22; ulema in, 83, 104, 105, 106, 114, 116–17, 119, 122. *See also* Indo-Pakistan subcontinent
Paša, Cevdet, 70, 77
Paša, Said, 62, 69
Paša, Ziya, 49, 90
Penal law, 2, 30, 31
Pesantrins, 46, 81, 82, 127
Peshwar, University of, 119, 121
Philosophy, 33, 123; at al-Azhar, 66, 67, 68, 100; critical history of Islamic, 148–49; in India, 35, 39–40; in Iran, 35, 45, 80, 106–7, 157; in medieval education, 33; and modernism, 73, 74; reconstruction of Islamic, 157–59; rejection of, 34–36, 135, 157–58; in Turkey, 95, 96. *See also* Metaphysics; Theology
Pīr-i-Rūmī wa Murīd-i-Hindī (Iqbāl), 57–58
Politics, 109, 139–40
Positivism, 132
Poverty, amelioration of, 16, 19, 90
Prayer, 21–22, 31
Punjab, University of the, 119, 121, 122

Qānūn (Ibn Sīnā), 40
Qiyās, 2, 18, 25–26, 101, 150
Qum, 31, 81, 107
Qurʾān, 48, 55, 77–78, 95, 138; appeal to individual verses of, 25–26, 101; commentaries and supercommentaries on, 17, 36–39, 40, 45, 63, 70, 103, 128, 145, 150–51; deduction of general principles from, 6, 20–22; defense of, 103; differing interpretations of, 144–45; and early generations, 23–25; ethics of, 154–57; firm and ambiguous verses of, 143; and fundamentalists, 141–43; and historical Islam, 2–7, 85–86, 141–47, 149, 150, 151–52; and history, study of, 160, 161–62; and Iqbāl's theology, 153–54; and Islamic metaphysics, 132–33, 143; and medieval education, 31, 35, 36–39, 40; need for understanding unity of, 1–11, 20–22, 101, 141, 142–43, 154; and neorevivalists, 137; purpose of commands by, 18–19, 27, 154; and rational knowledge, 34, 50–51, 52, 134–36, 158; and science of rhetoric and eloquence, 36, 39, 70; and "simplicity" of Islam, 117, 137; situational context of

commands by, 5–6, 17–19; and social morality, 5, 14–17, 19, 90, 108, 124, 128, 152–53; sociohistorical studies of, 96–97, 109; and Sufism, 27–28
Qureshī, Ishtiāq Ḥusain, 110–11, 115, 117, 121–22

Radhakrishnan, Sir S., 120
Rahman, Fazlur, 110, 111
Ratio legis, 5–6
Rational sciences, 33–35, 41. *See also* Islamic sciences; Science
Rāzī, Fakhr al-Dīn al-, 32, 152
Reconstruction of Religious Thought in Islam (Iqbāl), 132–33, 153–54
Revelation: and Ashʿarism, 27; occasions of (shu'un al-nuzūl), 16, 17, 128, 145; and Qurʾān, 1–2, 4, 5; and science, 51
Reza Khān, 80–81
Reza Shāh, 80, 105, 109
Ribā. *See* Usury
Risālat al-Tawḥīd (Muḥammad ʿAbduh), 100
Riẓā, Muḥammad, 41
Rodinson, Maxime, 16
Rūmī, Jalāl al-Dīn al-, 39, 57–58
Rüshdiye, 48, 59

Ṣabrī, Muṣṭafā, 70
Safarnāma (Shiblī Nuʿmānī), 130
Safavid dynasty, 31, 35, 79, 109
Saʿīdī, ʿAbd al-Mutaʿāl al-, 100
Ṣalāḥ al-Dīn Ayyūbī (Namik Kemāl), 53
Santillana, 32
Santri, 81
Saudi Arabia, 133
Schacht, J., 24
Science: at al-Azhar, 64, 67; and early modernists, 46–47, 49–52, 55–56; gap between Islamic nations and West, 72–73, 139; in Islamic research, 96; and Islamic values, 131–32. *See also* Islamic sciences; Technology
Science of rhetoric and eloquence, 36–37, 39, 70
Secularism, 15, 43, 47, 156, 159; of knowledge, 135; and neorevivalism, 137, and politics, 140; in Turkey, 47–49, 57–58, 98, 139–40, 156; of West, 15, 111–12, 133–34
Sedjarah Pendidikan Islam di Indonesia, 125
Seljukids, 31
Shāfiʿī, al-, 18, 26
Sharbīnī, al-, 66
Sharīʿa, 21, 32, 33, 43, 47, 101, 145, 156; and government, 29; and secular law, 29–31. *See also* Islamic law
Sharīʿātī, ʿAlī, 109
Sharīʿa University, 125
Shāṭibī, al-, 20–23, 30, 101
Shaybānī, al-, 25
Shiblī NuʿMānī, Muḥammad, 53, 56, 72, 78, 130, 153
Shīʿism, 3, 31, 103; and government, 29, 79, 104–5; in Iran, 35, 45, 79–81, 104–5, 107, 109, 157; theology of, 32–33
Shirāzī, Ṣadr al-Dīn al-, 35–36, 39
Shūrā-yi-Fatwā, 108
Shuʾun al-nuzūl (occasions of revelation), 16, 17, 128, 143, 145
Siddīqī, al-, 128
Sirhindī, al-, 14
Sirri, Selim, 61
Sind, University of the, 119, 121
Slavery, 19
Smith, W. Cantwell, 53
Socialism, 87–88, 127
Social sciences, 68, 73, 96–97, 131–32, 159–62
Sociology, 96–97, 98
Soviet Union, 44, 84, 111–12, 114
Spain, 53
Spiritualism, 127–28
Stalin, 131

State Institute for Islam, 126
Studies in Islam, 76
Successors, and Successors to the Successors, 24–25
Sufism, 3, 41, 76, 116–17, 133, 147, 152; critical history of, 148, 149; and intellectualism, 34, 39; in Pakistan, 45, 115; theology of, 14–15; and ulema, 39, 44, 56–57, 119, 149
Suhrawardī, al-, 39
Sulamī, ʿIzz al-Dīn Ibn ʿAbd al-Salām al-, 30
Sulayman the Magnificent, 35
Sunna: as background for understanding Qurʾān, 143, 146–48; and fundamentalists, 142; and Islamic law, 18, 20, 22–23, 29, 101; of Muḥammad's contemporaries, 17–18; need for study of, 117; and social morality, 15, 90
Sunnism, 29, 31, 42, 44, 80; and philosophy, 106–7, 109, 149; theology of, 3, 32. *See also* Islamic orthodoxy

Taftāzānī, al-, 32, 38
Tahānavī, al-, 37
Tahdhīb-i-akhlāq, 54
Tahṭwāwī, Rifāʿa al-, 63–64
Tanẓīmāt reformers, 47–49, 92, 96
Taqrīb bayn al-Madhāhīb, al-, 78–79
Taqwā, 155
Tarbiya, 53, 62
Technology: gap between Islamic nations and West, 73, 139; Iqbāl on, 57; and traditional culture, 88–89, 90, 113; "useful," 46–48, 49, 50. *See also* Science
Tevfik, Riza, 61
Tehran University, 108
Thānavī, Ashraf ʿAlī, 76–77
Theology, 96, 137, 157; Aḥmad Khān on reform of, 52; at al-Azhar, 100, 101, 138–39; critical history of, 148, 149–50, 151–52; development of, 26–28; and failure to understand Qurʾān as unity, 3–4; in medieval curriculum, 32–33, 35, 36, 39, 40, 41; systematic reconstruction of, 151–54, 155–56
Tjī, al-, 32
Tobacco Concessions, 79, 80, 105
Ṭufayl, Miān Muḥammad, 117
Turkey, 49–50, 53; and classical modernism, 47–49, 59–60, 61–63, 77, 78; and contemporary modernism, 85, 90, 91, 92–99, 104, 126, 138–39; madrasas in, 61, 62, 69–70, 92; medieval, 35, 37–38, 45; ulema in, 44–45, 59, 61–62, 94, 98; and West, 43–44, 54, 55, 87, 90
Ṭūsī, Nasīr al-Dīn al-, 33, 37

Ulema: al-Ẓawāhirī on, 65, 66; in Egypt, 44–45, 63, 79–80, 98, 103–4; in India, 44–45, 78–80; in Indonesia, 44–45, 46; and intellectualism, 34, 35–36; and Iqbāl, 120; in Iran, 44, 79–81, 104–6, 108–9; and modernization, 43, 44–45, 59, 63, 71, 73; and neorevivalists, 137; and Sharīʿa law, 30–31, 156; and Sufism, 39, 56–57, 119, 149; in Turkey, 44–45, 59, 61–62, 94, 98. *See also* Nadwat al-ʿUlamāʾ; Nahḍat al-ʿUlamāʾ
ʿUmar, 24
United States, 111–12
Urdu language, 70, 75
Usūlīs, 107
Usury, 16, 18, 30, 127, 136

Values: cognition of historical, 4–5, 10–11; and law, 15, 156; and science, 53–54, 131–32, 159–61; in secular society, 15, 28, 88–89, 133–34, 160

Vatan (Namik Kemāl), 53

Wahhābī movement, 99, 136, 141
Walīy Allāh, Shāh, 30, 40, 41, 45
Wansbrough, John, 103
West: and Islamic fundamentalism, 136, 142; Islamic scholarship of, 124, 149–50, 151; and morals, 28, 55, 86–87, 88–89, 133–34, 139; philosophy of, 96. *See also* Colonialism; Science; Technology
Whitehead, Alfred North, 131, 154
Women: education of, 61, 76–7 102; rights of, 18, 19, 127, 136, 153

Yaḥyā Khān, 115
Young Ottomans, 49

Zakāt, 16, 19, 31, 136
Zawāhirī, Muḥammad ibn Ibrāhīm al-, 64–66
Zāwiya, 39